7.95
11/18/05

QA
76.76
.H94
T5948
2004

SCHLINES

D1569114

ML

Other Books in Schaum's Easy Outlines Series Include:

SCHAUM'S *Easy* OUTLINES

XML

BASED ON SCHAUM'S
Outline of Theory and Problems of XML
BY ED TITTEL

ABRIDGEMENT EDITOR
DALE A. BROWN, Ph.D.

SCHAUM'S OUTLINE SERIES
McGRAW-HILL

New York   Chicago   San Francisco   Lisbon   London   Madrid
Mexico City   Milan   New Delhi   San Juan
Seoul   Singapore   Sydney   Toronto

The McGraw·Hill Companies

ED TITTEL has been an instructor at Austin Community College since 1996. He teaches markup languages and networking topics. The author of over 100 computer books and the originator of the Exam Cram certification preparation series, he also teaches various Window topics at the NetWorld + Interop trade show.

DALE A. BROWN has been a Professor of Computer Science at The College of Wooster since 1987, teaching courses in introductory and intermediate programming, computer organization, database technology, machine intelligence, and theory of computation. He received his masters and Ph.D. degrees from Syracuse University.

1 2 3 4 5 6 7 8 9 0 DOC DOC 0 9 8 7 6 5 4

ISBN 0-07-142245-5

Contents

Chapter 1
AN OVERVIEW
OF XML

Origins of XML

The Extensible Markup Language (XML) emerged in 1996 as a subset of the Standard Generalized Markup Language (SGML). The design goals in the original World Wide Web Consortium (W3C) XML Working Draft document described a software-readable markup language that integrated easily with existing markup languages, such as HTML and SGML, and was easily readable by humans. In February 1998, XML 1.0 reached W3C Recommendation Status. A January 2000 update of HTML incorporated some basic features of XML with the release of the Extensible Hypertext Markup Language (XHTML).

What makes XML so special? The key lies in XML's name itself—the Extensible Markup Language. The word *extensible* reflects that the language is flexible, scalable, and adaptable. One can "extend" the information in a set of data by defining new tags that identify particular components in that data. XML data can take whatever form is necessary for distribution of information, either over the Web or between software applications. The constraints and limitations of HTML do not apply.

Remember

The term *markup* describes a process of identifying the different elements of a document so that a program or person can process them. For instance, web designers use HTML markup tags, like `<br>`, `<head>`, and `</head>`, to identify elements for interpretation by a browser.

XML provides two means of establishing new tags to identify elements of the data: Document Type Definitions (DTDs) and schema documents. By coupling XML documents with a DTD or a schema, it is possible to define markup tags (or element identifiers) in unique and specific ways. One can customize such tags to meet a particular need and structure while enabling information exchange in a language through which both software and humans can easily interact. By creating rules and elements to meet the needs of the task, XML allows the exchange of structured data in an accessible yet easy-to-read format.

Data searching and retrieval is an area of tremendous growth and research regarding HTML. As anyone who has used search engines knows, search phrasing is somewhat a "dark science." It seems that searches frequently recover either too little or too much information, depending on the user's skill, luck, or patience. The fundamental problem is that a given word has many different meanings, depending upon the context in which it appears. Users need a way to identify the meaning of a word by knowing both its spelling and the context in which it appears. In HTML, one uses meta elements to mark keywords, dates, and so on, but this method is weak because of the small number of available meta elements and the unlimited variations of data that can occur. By contrast, XML permits the definition of new tags to match any new type of data. It therefore enables context-dependent searching.

The designers of XML had several initial objectives. They desired:

- A content-driven language derived from and compatible with SGML
- Tools for Electronic Data Interchange (EDI) and other data-driven applications that HTML lacked
- Platform-independence
- The capability of distributing data over the Web through the browser
- The capability of distributing data over the Web through means other than the browser.

Differences between XML and HTML

Although HTML, XML, and (their hybrid) XHTML all use markup tags as containers for data elements and appear on the surface to be quite similar, the tags themselves are quite different, not only in definition and meaning, but also in their methods of creation and specification. Whereas HTML and its successor, XHTML, use elements that are more or less universally defined and accepted as HTML 4.01 or XHTML 1.0 (via the implied DTD that the browser includes), XML allows, encourages, and thrives on elements that some user or group has created for structuring data to a specific intent and purpose. If an element is required for XML and is not part of the DTD, the author can create the element needed and define it as an add-on.

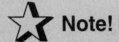

Note!

Don't confuse *tags* and *elements*. The information:
`<title> Outline of XML </title>`
is an element while `<title>` is the opening tag
and `</title>` is the closing tag.

At the core, the differences between HTML and XML are very simple: HTML is a *presentation* markup language, readable and rendered by almost any modern Web browser, whereas XML is a *content* markup language, with no inherent, or built-in, presentation elements, only content-definition elements.

XML allows one to design elements as an application-specific process, defined in a schema or DTD, and used over the Web in a language that best describes the data itself. Definition of the necessary XML elements accomplishes a number of otherwise difficult tasks of context clarification. Again, XML defines the data, and HTML defines the presentation. To put it another way, XML processes data, whereas HTML displays data.

As even a casual user of HTML knows, most of the HTML elements influence the layout and look of the document—the presentation. Web professionals are all very familiar with such elements as `center` or `font`. These elements (and other presentation elements) do not indicate the type of data contained. Only a few HTML elements do this. For Web pages, this is generally adequate, and use of these elements will continue to grow and thrive as the Web continues to expand. However, for indicating the type of data or their purpose, HTML falls a bit short with its minuscule number of content-related elements.

You Need to Know

HTML combines information about both *content* and *presentation* format. XML consists only of content information. If it is necessary to present the data, presentation format is the responsibility of other support software.

Because XML is a content markup language, it is necessary to specify only the actual data contained in the tags. For example, one might wish to create a list of books that consists of the title, the author, the subject, the publisher, and more. There are no HTML elements to specify that the enclosed text is the name of the author.

XML does not have these limitations. The document's creator is relatively free to create the needed elements in a DTD or a schema that the reading software or agent can access. The story does not end here, however. Because XML is content-driven, it is necessary to provide a separate method for presentation. Later chapters discuss this fully. Suffice it to say here that one combines the XML document with a *style sheet* via the Extensible Stylesheet Language (XSL) or Cascading Style Sheets (CSS). The style sheet defines how to present the content of each element. The best part is that, for software or agents that do not require presentation markup, one can simply provide the XML and the content it contains. Simple exchange of XML data does not necessitate presentation.

Note!

XML requires that the author create *well-formed* documents; that is, documents that properly match starting and closing tags and abide by logical rules of nesting. Most XML software will also *validate a document* by checking to make sure that the document uses tags only in a manner that is consistent with its DTD or schema.

Here are some of the key differences between XML and HTML:

- XML is a *content* markup language; HTML is a *presentation* markup language.
- XML allows user-defined elements; HTML elements are predefined.
- XML usually requires validation; in HTML, almost anything goes.
- XML is data-driven; HTML is display-driven.
- XML allows data exchange between software applications without the need for presentation information; HTML is designed for visual presentation.
- XML is strictly defined and interpreted; HTML is very loosely interpreted. XML elements must be closed; in HTML, empty elements do not need to be closed.
- XML is case sensitive; HTML is not.

Uses of XML

Early uses of XML include documents for traditional Web browsers and industry specific document exchange. Industries and disciplines such as chemistry, mathematics, real estate, weather observation, banking, electronic data interchange (EDI), and many more offer a vast potential use of XML. Because a DTD or schema defines the XML document to be specific to the needs of the users, XML can easily support any type of industry. For example, in the weather observation industry, the DTD or schema can provide the elements needed for wind speed, pressure, temperature, humidity, and so on. Observer systems can record the data, format it according to the element definitions, and forward it for interpretation by forecasting systems. Because each element defines a particular type of content and its formatting rules, the documents are mutually understood and easily readable by a human. If the XML ultimately requires presentation by a Web browser or other agent, the person responsible for presentation specifies the necessary XSL or CSS style sheet as well as rules for presentation; this encourages strictly defined elements and very narrow application within a specific industry or academic field. Many DTDs and schemas already exist for these applications, and others are being created constantly. XML will continue to evolve as more and more uses are discovered and implemented.

Wireless applications press XML into service in novel and very practical ways. The need to conserve bandwidth for and format information on a small, handheld screen cries out for simple, customizable data exchange media. XML can pass pure data or provide minimal presentation markup without all the excess baggage of HTML. Many flavors of XML will develop to meet the very narrow criteria of wireless display but expand into fully presented Web pages when the application requires it. The XML concept of separation between content and presentation is ideal in such circumstances.

XML Document Structure

Previous sections have emphasized that XML describes content rather than format. An XML document holds information, not a description of how to display that information. However, the information takes two different forms:

- *Logical structure* defines the units and subunits of the data containers (the elements) and the components they contain.
- *Physical structure* provides the data that goes into the elements. They include text, images, or other media, as allowed by the logical structure.

Consider the following subset of an XML document:

```
<letter>
      <greeting>
      Hello there
      </greeting>
</letter>
```

It forms a letter that contains a greeting that, in this case, consists of the string "Hello There." The tag information (`<letter>`, `<greeting>`, `</greeting>`, and `</letter>`) describes logical structure, while the string, `"Hello there,"` represents physical structure. The physical structure is the raw data, and the logical structure adds meaning to the physical structure by establishing its context. Without the logical structure in the tags, the characters are simply a string. With markup, it constitutes a greeting that is part of a letter.

The addition of more logical structure to the above markup generates a complete XML document:

```
<?xml version="1.0" standalone="yes"
      encoding ="UTF-8"?>
<letter>
      <greeting>
          Hello there
      </greeting>
</letter>
```

The new markup indicates that the document is using XML 1.0, that there is not an external DTD (`standalone="yes"`), and that the document is using `UTF-8` encoding for its characters. Following this *XML processing instruction* is the *opening root tag* (`<letter>`), which is followed by the rest of the document and the *closing root tag* (`</letter>`). Components, `version` and `standalone`, are *attributes* of the `xml` markup. Attributes specify property values of the elements within whose markup they exist. They have both names and values. In this case, the `xml` element has value `"1.0"` for the attribute with name `version` and value `"yes"` for the attribute with name `standalone`. As in the example, an XML document specifies an attribute's value in the opening tag for the element that contains it. For a document to be well-formed, attribute values must have quotation marks around them.

The physical structure of an XML document is the structure of the actual data and information. XML documents that share a logical structure, as defined by the schema or DTD, can vary dramatically in physical structure, based on the data they contain. In the preceding example, the logical structure `<greeting...</greeting>` could contain "Hello there" or some other greeting as the physical structure.

Notice the nesting of the elements in the document. The `<greeting ... greeting>` tag pair nests within `<letter>...</letter>`. This careful attention to the nesting of elements is part of what makes a well-formed XML document.

Consider the addition of a few simple elements to the example:

```
<?xml version= "1. 0" standalone= "yes"
    encoding= "UTF-8" ?>
<letter>
    <greeting Hello World! </greeting>
    <signature>
        <message>
        Most Sincerely...
        </message>
        <name>
        Joe Smith
        </name>
    </signature>
</letter>
```

Again, notice the nesting as emphasized by the indentation.

The letter contains both a greeting and a signature, and signature contains both a message and a name. Therefore, this is a well-formed document. If any of the element tags are out of sequence, for example, if the closing message tag and the opening name tags are transposed or overlap, the document is not well-formed. As a further requirement of being well-formed, all attribute names should be unique. Finally, all elements should be closed, whether in pairs, as in this example, or as empty tags, such as `<subject name= "example XML"/>`. Notice the slash and closing bracket (/ >). This creates a single but complete tag. The familiar <br> tag in HTML would now take the form <br / > to be correct in XML. Note that for backwards compatibility reasons, there must be a space before the closing slash in XHTML. An example would be <br / >.

Note!

XML and its related software applications ignore indentation. The illustrations in this outline use indentation simply to enhance the reader's understanding of the markup.

Another important aspect of XML document structure is the use of *entitie*s. These represent reserved sequences of characters used to distinguish regular text from markup. For example, the left angle bracket (<) identifies the beginning of a tag in markup. Therefore, if the goal is for the parser (browser) to display a left angle bracket and not render it as markup, it is necessary to use the bracket entity. In this case, the correct entity is <.

Entity references begin with an ampersand (&) and end with a semicolon (;). To use an entity, one can reference it by its unique name. Entity declarations enable the association of a name with some other fragment of content that can be part of regular text, part of the DTD, or a reference to an external file containing either text or binary data. The current discussion deals only with predefined entities. Table 1-1 lists the five predefined entity characters.

Table 1-1 The Five Predefined Entity Characters

HTML	Character	Description
>	>	Greater than
<	<	Less than
&	&	Ampersand
&apos,	`	Apostrophe
"	"	Double quote

These entities serve in instances where their corresponding symbols represent themselves rather than markup symbols. Of course, it is possible to declare other entities, but these are the only ones built into XML.

You Need to Know

The basic rules of creating well-formed documents are:

    a. Begin the XML document with a declaration.

    b. Provide at least one element (the root element) that contains all other elements.

    c. Nest tags correctly.

    d. Use both start and end tags for elements that are not empty, and close empty tags properly.

    e. Quote all attribute values.

Unless a document is well-formed, it will not parse correctly, and it can cause an error on the parser; therefore, well-formed XML should be a fundamental goal at all times.

DTDs

A Document Type Definition (DTD) can provide element meaning, attributes, logical structure, and context. It extends logical structure definition beyond the minimal standards of well-formed documents. A DTD defines the elements and their attributes that specialize XML to specific disciplines and uses. It also enables exchange and accessibility by other software. A DTD is a set of rules that explicitly define the name, content, and context of each element. Therefore, a DTD can serve as the foundation of an XML document, defining the template for processing images, links, and other entities.

The DTD defines the building blocks (elements) that the XML document can use. It is possible to declare a DTD in-line as part of the XML document or in an external file referenced in the document through a *Uniform Resource Identifier* (URI). External files are common when the DTD is complex or when the DTD defines a common standard used by multiple individuals for information exchange.

Subsequent chapters will illustrate this material in greater detail. The purpose here is to get a better sense of the essentials of DTD creation and the use of DTDs in an XML document. The basic building blocks of a DTD are as follows:

- *Elements.* The main blocks of the document, such as `body` or `head`, and `xml`.
- *Attributes.* Information to further describe an element, such as `<body text="#000000">`. Each attribute has a name and a value, as specified in the opening tag for the element than contains it.
- *Entities.* Variables that describe certain common text references.
- *PCDATA.* This means *parsed character data*. Think of PCDATA as the text contained between the start and end tags of an XML element. PCDATA is text that the parser will treat as markup. Where appropriate, it will expand its entities.
- *CDATA.* This means *character data*; the parser virtually ignores the text contained in a CDATA tag. It simply copies it intact, neither parsing nor expanding it, even if it contains markup symbols.

Fortunately, it is most often not necessary to create a DTD from scratch. XML authors and creators can refer to and access may DTDs that already exist. Most are specific to the needs and practices of a particular discipline, organization, or company. There are many DTD repositories and references on the Web.

Because the language used is very simple, it is quite easy to master the actual DTD syntax; additionally, it is very useful to examine some common ones.

> # Remember
>
> DTDs consist of two key components: the *element* and the *attribute*. These two ingredients are essential to describing content.

In a DTD, XML elements reside within ELEMENT declarations. The syntax is either < ! ELEMENT element-name category> or < ! ELEMENT element-name (element-content) >. The usual structure of a DTD begins with a definition of the root element. It then defines all elements used in the root element, but not previously defined. It continues defining referenced elements that do not have previous definitions until it has defined all elements that are present. Here is a sample DTD for the example letter document:

```
<!ELEMENT letter (greeting, signature)>
<!ELEMENT greeting (#PCDATA)>
<!ELEMENT signature (message, name)>
<!ELEMENT message (#PCDATA)>
<!ELEMENT name (#PCDATA)>
```

If an element has attributes, they too require declaration. For example, the author might have defined element letter to have an attribute specifying a letter-type with possible values "B" for business and "F" for friend and default value friend:

```
<!ELEMENT letter (greeting, signature)>
<!ATTLIST letter letter-type (B,F) "F">.
<!ELEMENT greeting (#PCDATA)>
<!ELEMENT signature (message, name)>
<!ELEMENT message (#PCDATA)>
<!ELEMENT name (#PCDATA)>
```

Chapter 2 will provide more thorough examples of DTD usage.

> ## ⭐ Note!
>
> DTDs were the original means for defining logical structure in XML documents. Probably the major weakness of DTDs is that they are not, in themselves, XML documents.

Schemas

Relative to the DTD, the XML schema represents an improved, but substantially more complex, mechanism for defining XML structure. XML schemas identify a set of components in XML documents and provide the rules for their correct combination. A schema is an XML-based alternative to a DTD. Like DTDs, schemas define the following:

- Elements that appear in a document
- Attributes that appear in a document
- Elements that are child elements
- The sequence in which the child elements can appear
- The number of child elements
- Whether an element is empty or can include text
- Default values for attributes.

All of this information is present in a DTD, but as intended successors to DTDs, schemas are supposed to implement them more effectively. Some of the reasons that the W3C recommends XML schemas are as follows:

- They are easier to learn than DTDs.
- They are extensible to future additions.
- They are richer than DTDs.
- They support data types.
- They support namespaces.
- They are written in XML.

XML schemas improve on DTDs in several ways, including the use of XML syntax and support for data types and namespaces, both of which are invaluable for interfacing XML and databases. There are many instances in which a schema may be preferable to a DTD, but schemas are not intended to fully replace the DTD. In fact, there are many instances in which a DTD may be a better choice. For example, if the data type is not critical, a DTD might be more economical to define and use, or perhaps a very workable DTD is already in place; therefore, the small advantage gained by the stricter schema might be negated by the current widespread use of a DTD.

If one is creating a brand new XML application, it is appropriate to evaluate the available options. Schemas offer distinct advantages over DTDs in the area of data typing. For example, it is easy to require a negative integer value as opposed to a simple integer value or to define XML data to have same data type as a database field. Schemas allow a much more thorough description of the data contained in an XML document, but they also require a much more thorough design.

Remember

A DTD might be preferable to a schema if:

   a. It is necessary to use a compact definition

   b. The data is primarily prose or readable text

   c. Nesting is more important than data typing

   d. The tools available do not support schemas

Validation

Validation of an XML document is the process of verifying that it follows the structure defined in its DTD or schema. Formal validation is something that might be new to most HTML authors because it is not needed in order to create viewable and usable HTML documents. For the most part, if a document displays properly in a Web browser, it is somewhat valid. Some browsers might tolerate minor errors better than others, but the fact that a target browser displays the data constitutes a crude form of validation. Keep in mind, however, that software agents must process an XML document, and a program's tolerance for errors or ambiguity is much less than a human's. If there are flaws in the markup or it is incomplete, the document can fail to process correctly. Therefore, XML documents must validate in addition to being well-formed.

Typically, the entity that validates a DTD-based XML document is a program called an XML parser. The parser attempts to read and interpret the document by following several steps. First, it verifies that the document is well-formed. If not, the parser quits and returns an error. The parser then compares the document to the DTD, which the document has specified using a DOCTYPE declaration like the following:

```
<!DOCTYPE xml-example SYSTEM "xml-example.dtd">
```

The DTD must be accessible to the document in question, either locally or through a URI. The referenced DTD must accurately describe all elements in the document or the document fails validation.

Validation for documents using a schema instead of a DTD is very similar. First, the document must be well-formed. Then an XML Schema parser, such as IBM's *XML Schema Quality Checker*, compares the document to the referenced schema and tests it for validity. Failure again causes termination of the process and an error return.

There are many parsers available for XML validation. For DTD-based XML, SAX and its derivatives are the de facto standard. SAX is a Java-based tool, and it is therefore quite portable to many platforms. XML parsers exist for most popular programming languages, such as C, C++, Python, Perl, and others. Xerces, for example, is a C++ parser designed by and available from the Apache group (http://xml.apache.org/). A common tool is the MSXML parser available from Microsoft and introduced in Internet Explorer 5.0.

Namespaces

XML uses the concept of *namespaces* to avoid conflicts that arise when a page imports definitions from more than one source. In such circumstances, it is possible to have multiple definitions for a single name. The use of namespaces permits the XML author to specify which definition to use or to guarantee that the later addition of a duplicate definition will not cause any conflicts.

In HTML, `title` tags mark up the section of text to appear in the browser title bar. There is no confusion here. However, what if the purpose is to combine two XML documents that both use a `title` element in different contexts, and neither of them relates to the HTML `title` element? Assume, for example, that the general topic of the document is books on genealogy, all of which have a book element, `title`. Also assume that the books deal with family history, including royal families, which also have a `title` as part of the name element. How does one separate the book title from the royal `title` from the Web page `title`? It is possible to impose upper and lower case naming conventions to solve the problem, but this is a brittle and artificial fix. A better solution is to use a namespace to define which `title` element definition is appropriate.

Defining a namespace requires a few new XML declarations. The examples that follow illustrate the namespace syntax used in XML 1.0:

```
<royalty:title
  xmlns:royalty="http://www.royalty.com/xml" />
<genealogy:title
  xmlns:genealogy="http://www.geneal.com/xml" />
```

In this way, the document uses the URI of each namespace to declare the sources of the different title definitions. To use the different namespace versions, it is only necessary to include the tag with the name using one of the forms, `<royalty:title>` or `<genealogy:title>`. It would be a good idea to add a declaration for `<html:title>` to guarantee consistency and completeness.

For a full discussion of namespaces, see one of the many online resources, such as the W3C's "Namespaces in XML Recommendation" at www.w3.org/TR/xml-names11/.

Comments

Comments in an XML document are more important than in most standard HTML documents—more along the lines of comments placed in mainstream programming languages such as Java or Visual Basic. The need for comments while learning XML is of great importance, and a succinct, readable commenting style is key to maintaining legible and understandable markup. It is very easy for an author to forget the purpose and function of some simple task that was familiar when it was designed but which later seems to make no sense.

The syntax for comments in XML is very much like HTML and XHTML. XML uses the familiar < ! -- to start a comment and --> to end it. The same rules apply here as in the other markup languages:

- Comments may not appear inside any markup.
- Comments may not end with ---> (three hyphens).
- One can automatically create multi-line comments with one open and one closing tag.
- A double hyphen should not appear in any markup so as to maintain consistency with the comment syntax.
- The parser treats markup inside a comment as text rather than parsing it: `<!--start the <root> element -->`.

Remember

The only XML markup not translated in some way by the parser is text that is within comments or that is within a CDATA section.

Processing Instructions

Processing instructions (PIs) contain instructions for an application that is processing an XML document. PIs have a target that identifies the target application, followed by the instructions. All PIs start with < ? and they close with ?>. PIs can indicate instructions that an application must process. Many PIs specify a style sheet (XSLT) for integration with the XML document. Like comments, PIs do not generate rendered output. Instead, they request processing by the indicated application and possibly provide information to it.

The author may place PIs anywhere in a document. The PI is similar to a server-side include instruction in HTML or a meta element directive, that is, instructions for a robot or other application that encounters the XML document.

To specify a style sheet, one would write a PI similar to:

```
<?xml-stylesheet href="mystylesheet.css"
      type="text/css"?>
```

This looks remarkably like the style directive used in HTML, with the `type` and `href` both declared. The `href` path follows conventional URI rules. The following is an example of PIs for robots:

```
<?robots index="yes|no" follow="yes|no"?>
```

Any information that an XML file must provide to an application that might process the file must reside in a PI. Multiple PIs are allowed, Further information is available in the W3C document, "Associating Style Sheets with XML Documents, Version 1.0" (www.w3.org/TR/xml-stylesheet/). Below are some examples of style sheet directives from that document with their HTML counterparts. These are style sheet directives. The XML PI is given first, followed by the HTML 4.0 equivalent.

XML:
```
<?xml-stylesheet href="mystyle.css"
      type="text/css"?>
```
HTML:
```
<link href="mystyle.css" rel="stylesheet"
      type="text/css">
```
XML:
```
<?xml-stylesheet href="mystyle.css"
      title="Compact" type="text/css"?>
```

HTML:

```
<link href="mystyle.css" title="Compact"
     rel="stylesheet" type="text/css">
```

XML:

```
<?xml-stylesheet alternate="yes"
     href="mystyle.css" title="Medium"
     type="text/css"?>
```

HTML:

```
<link href="mystyle.css" title="Medium"
     rel="alternate stylesheet"
     type="text/css">
```

Looking at these closely, it becomes apparent that the XML is quite familiar to HTML authors, and very little rethinking is needed to put it into practice.

xml:lang **and** xml:space

The two attributes of the XML namespaces are xml:lang and xml:space. Both are unique to XML. They are the keys to document presentation and readability. The xml:space attribute preserves white space in the physical layout, and xml:lang provides a mechanism for text translation and presentation in a localized character set.

The xml:lang attribute creates a mechanism for an XML document to contain multi-language text and to present documents with internationalized versions, including built-in translations. The xml:lang attribute allows the author to translate the XML to a specified character set. Each element potentially can have a different xml:lang attribute, although in practice this would not make much sense.

To use the xml:lang attribute, emulate these examples:

```
<quote xml:lang="en">
  <!-- This is a quote in English -->
  Time flies...
</quote>

<quote xml:lang="la">
  <!-- This is a quote in Latin-->
  Tempus fugit...
</quote>
```

The language code specified is a two-letter designation that is defined in ISO 639, "Codes for the Representation of Languages" (www. oasis-open.org/cover/iso639a.html). Well over 400 languages are already specified, and if this is not enough, one can create new ones.

White space has been a problem for many versions of HTML because of the inherent HTML tendency to reduce white space characters down to one space no matter how many are present. This impacts spaces, blanks, tabs, and so on. The only option for HTML authors has been the entity , but this requires five characters to conserve one, not a very economical tradeoff. In XML, there is an easy way to maintain this otherwise lost white space. One may attach this special attribute to an element to signal the intention that the application should preserve white space for that element. Valid documents that wish to use it must declare xml:space, like any other attribute.

To maintain white space within a document, use the xml:space attribute in conjunction with XSL or CSS and as an attribute declaration:

```
<!ATTLIST element xml:space
    (default|preserve) "default">
```

or

```
<!ATTLIST element xml:space
    (default|preserve) "preserve">
```

One declares this as part of an element declaration in standard fashion. The treatment of xml:space depends on the application being used. Ideally, any document that specifies preserve should render verbatim, with all white spaces (tabs, spaces, etc.) left in place, but this is agent-dependent. The default behavior is to replace all sequences of white space characters with a single space.

XML Tools

The following are available CSS editors, together with the platform on which each runs:

css-mode	Emacs
HTML-Kit	Win32
Dtddoc	Python

DTDParse	Perl
LiveDTD	Perl
Per1SGM	Perl

The following are available DTD editors, together with the platform on which each runs:

EzDTD	Win32
tdtd	Emacs

The following are available DTD generators, together with the platform on which each runs:

Data Descriptors by Example	Java
FirstSTEP	Win32
Rhythmyx XspLit	Win32
SAXON	Java
XMI Toolkit	Java 1.2

The following are available DTD parsers, together with the platform on which each runs:

CL-XML Common	Lisp
DTDParser	Java
DTDParser	Perl
PXP	Objective Caml 3.00
xmlproc	Python 1.5

The integrated development environments (IDEs), XML, and Web Services DE run on Win32.

The schema converter, DTD2RELAX, runs on Java.

The following are available XSL checkers, together with the platform on which each runs:

XSL Lint	Perl
XSL Trace	Java

The XSL converters, XSL to XSLT Converter, runs on Win32.

The following are available XSL editors, together with the platform on which each runs:

HTML-Kit	Win32
XPath Tester	Java 1.2
XSL Editor	Java
XSL Tester	Win32
xslide	Emacs

The following are available XSLT generators, together with the platform on which each runs:

Rhythmyx XspLit	Win32
WH2FO	Java

Chapter 2
DOCUMENT TYPE DEFINITIONS

Document Type Declarations

Every Extensible Markup Language (XML) document needs a blueprint, a foundation that defines what each element in the document means and what is appropriate, proper, and understood within the context of the XML document. By definition, XML encourages the custom use and definition of tags; therefore, it is necessary to have some means of establishing the tags and the other structure that identify every new element.

The currently most common tool for element declaration is the *Document Type Definition* (DTD). The DTD has been in use since the Standard Generalized Markup Language (SGML, developed in 1988). The Hypertext Markup Language (HTML) and its derivatives use DTDs rather transparently since the browser refers to them, but the user never sees them. XML has brought common use of the DTD back to the forefront of Web development.

In the XML processing instruction (also called the *prolog*), the author defines the document to be of one of two types: *standalone* (standalone="yes") or *not standalone* (standalone="no"). Standalone documents do *not* require a DTD. The default value of the standalone attribute is "no", which requires that a DTD be present.

A DTD can be either *internal* or *external*. An external DTD takes the form of an ASCII (American Standard Code for Information Interchange) text file with the file extension, *.DTD*. The author specifies an external DTD using a Uniform Resource Identifier (URI) in the prologue. An internal DTD resides within the document type (DOCTYPE) declaration. DTDs used in this way are available for reference only within the specific document.

The DTD is the key to element meaning. It establishes attributes, logical structure, and context for the XML document. The DTD defines the elements and the attributes they require and enables exchange of the document and interpretation of it by other software. A DTD is a set of rules that explicitly define the name, content, and context of each element. Therefore, the DTD is the foundation of an XML document, defining the template for how each image, link, and all other entities are processed. It is required for an XML document to be valid as opposed to just well formed.

The DTD defines the building blocks (elements) that the XML document can use. The author can declare the DTD in-line or as an external document, or the XML can have no DTD. One of the great benefits of the DTD system is that it allows the XML document to carry its own format description along with it or to use a commonly available DTD via a URI. Often XML documents that are interchanged within a specific industry or academic discipline will share a common DTD, developed specifically for that purpose. Centralized repositories for DTDs are becoming more commonplace, whether as URIs on the Web or limited to a local-area network (LAN).

> # Remember
>
> Without a DTD or a schema, there is no way to validate a document. Validation *means* conformity to a schema or DTD.

The following pages discuss the basic DTD building blocks:

- *Elements*. The main components of HTML and XML.
- *Tags*. Characters used to enclose the elements.
- *Attributes*. Information that further describes an element.
- *Notations*. References to helper applications or plug-ins.
- *Entities*. Variables to describe common text references.
- *PCDATA*. Parsed character data, which is the text between an XML element's start and end tags.
- *CDATA*. Character data, indicated by the CDATA tag. This data is not parsed.

The example used here for investigation of the above topics is a motion picture DTD. Many authors find it helpful to create a simple outline of the DTD before implementing it. For the motion picture DTD, the following list of desired information offers a starting point:

- Title
- Year
- Genre
- Director
- Distributor
- Cast
- Music
- Run time
- Country
- Language
- Medium
- Certification

Each of these items *might* represent an element. Elements are essential to DTDs and XML because they provide the logical structure of the document. The element provides the skeletal foundation and components of the XML document. Each element contains the *name* of the element, any *attributes* it possesses, and the *datatype* it contains.

An element has a *start tag,* nearly identical to those found in HTML, and an *end tag*, a tag that contains a slash (/). Recall that HTML permits empty tags (starting tags without closing tags) like <br>. Although XML also permits empty tags, it requires that they also be closed in the sense that they include a slash at the end, as in <br / >. One can also use opening and closing tags with empty elements (
</br>), but this occurs only rarely.

The basic element declaration has the following form:

```
<!ELEMENT element_name (datatype)>
```

An element can contain attributes, which are name-value pairs within a tagged element that modify certain features of the element. An attribute specifies the type (and value) of additional information about the element. For XML, quotation marks enclose all attribute values. Either single or double quotation marks are acceptable, but consistency enhances document quality. Attribute definitions reside in the DTD as a subset of the element definition. The syntax for the attribute is very similar to the element:

```
<!ATTLIST element_name attribute_name type
    default_value>
```

The motion picture example will declare a motionpicture for each film. This takes the form:

```
<!ELEMENT motionpicture (title, year, genre,
    director, cast, music)>
```

It declares that the motionpicture element contains the following other elements: title, year, genre, director, cast, and music.

Note!

Although XML requires that quotation marks enclose all attribute values, either single or double quotation marks are acceptable.

The validation process first verifies that it is working with a well-formed document and then parses the document by comparing to the DTD. It inspects all elements and other components and the relationships between them. Validation assures that all the elements are present and properly identified and that the overall logical structure is sound. If there are any errors or omissions, the parser will indicate this and either return an error or fail to display the document correctly. The comparison/validation process is especially critical during document exchange between software applications.

Table 2-1 describes some special symbols used in DTD definitions to qualify the number of occurences of objects within an element.

Table 2-1 Some Common Symbols Used in DTD Construction

Symbol	Definition
?	One or none
*	Wildcard: one, many, or none
+	At least one required, many allowed
,	Separates list items
|	Alternation (either or)
&	Entity
%	Parameter_entity

Table 2-2 summarizes the use of the symbols.

Table 2-2 Element components in rules

Component	Example	Description
`#PCDATA`	`<motionpicture` `(#PCDATA)>`	A `motionpicture` element contains parsed character data or text.
`#PCDATA,` `element-name`	`<motionpicture` `(#PCDATA, title)>`	Contains parsed character data and another element named title. `#PCDATA` always appears first in a rule. In this case, the comma inside the rule indicates that `motionpicture` *must* contain text and the title element.

`,` `(comma)`	`<motionpicture`
	`(title, year,`
	`genre)>`
		When commas separate two or more arguments, it indicates their order.

`|` `(bar or`
`pipe)`
	`motionpicture`
	`(title | year |`
	`genre)>`
		The pipe symbol specifies *either/or*. In this case, `motionpicture` has one of: title, year, or genre.

`Any valid`
`name`
`(by itself)`
	`<motionpicture`
	`(title)>`
		When an element occurs by itself it must occur exactly once. Here `motionpicture` must contain a title, used exactly once.

Table 2-2 Continued

? (question mark)	`<motionpicture (title, year?, genre?)>`	With a question mark, one can use the marked element(s) either zero or one times. Here `motionpicture` must contain `title` exactly once, followed by zero or one `year`, and zero or one `genre` elements.
+ (plus sign)	`<motionpicture (title+, year?, genre)>`	With a plus sign, one can use the marked element(s) either one or one times. Here `motionpicture` must contain `title` at least once.
* (asterisk)	`<motionpicture (title*, year?, genre)>`	With an asterisk, one can use the marked element(s) zero or more times. Here `motionpicture` can contain `title` zero or more times
() (parentheses)	`<motionpicture (#PCDATA|title)*>`	Parentheses define groupings, and may be multiple levels deep. Here `motionpicture` contains zero or more uses of *either* or *both* parsed character data and `title` elements.

The author can use the keyword #REQUIRED to indicate that a value for an attribute must be present with the data of the element or the keyword #IMPLIED to indicate that it is optional. A third possible keyword is #FIXED, which requires all instances of the element to contain a particular value. Table 2-3 illustrates the variety of DTD attribute types and provides sample usage of these keywords.

Table 2-3 Attributes Types

Attribute Type	Example	Description
CDATA	`<!ATTLIST genre category CDATA #REQUIRED>`	Character data holds text that the parser accepts without checking it. The genre element has an attribute named category. This attribute contains letters, numbers, or punctuation symbols and is required.
NMTOKEN	`<!ATTLIST genre category NMTOKEN #REQUIRED>`	Name token is text with some restrictions. The value contains numbers and letters. It cannot begin with the letters xml, and the only punctuation symbols it can contain are: -, ., and :. The genre element has a required attribute named category. This attribute contains a name token.
VALUE-LIST	`<!ATTLIST genre category (drama | scifi | comedy | other) "other">`	A value list provides a set of acceptable options for which the parser will check. It is a good idea to allow a default value like other.

Table 2-3. Continued

ID	`<!ATTLIST genre category ID #IMPLIED`	A attribute of type ID holds a unique identifier for the element. In this example, element genre has an ID value named category.
IDREF	`<!ATTLIST genre subGenre IDREF #IMPLIED`	The attribute type IDREF permits one element instance to refer to another instance with a value of type ID. Assuming that there is already a genre instance with category ID, "Q1", the example permits one to define a new genre instance: `<genre category="Q2" subGenre="Q1">` An instance may also reference an element of a different type.
ENTITY	`<!ATTLIST genre category ENTITY #IMPLIED`	An ENTITY attribute takes a value that the user has previously defined as an ENTITY. (See the discussion below on Notations)

Notations

The principle use for a NOTATION is to associate a name with a *helper application* or a *plug-in* to process a file. For example, if a special image file required a viewer program to access it, then one could create a named object that contains the location of the program. Assume that the DTD defines an element with an ENTITY attribute whose value might require processing by the viewer:

```
<!ELEMENT map EMPTY>
<!ATTLIST map image ENTITY #REQUIRED>
```

The XML document could then use a NOTATION to associate the location of the processing program with the name png

```
<!NOTATION png SYSTEM
    "file:///C:/Program Files/mapviewer.exe">
```

Additionally, the document might define an ENTITY to associate the name map1.png with the file at location http://www. anysite.net/map1.png and to indicate that the parser should invoke the program associated with the name png to process it. The (keyword NDATA tells the parser that the file is not an XML file and that the program named after it should do the processing:

```
<!ENTITY map1.png SYSTEM
    "http://www.anysite.net/map1.png"
    NDATA png>
```

Following are the DTD instructions in sequence:

```
<!ELEMENT map EMPTY>
<!ATTLIST map image ENTITY #REQUIRED>
<!NOTATION png SYSTEM
    "file:///C:/Program Files/mapviewer.exe">
<!ENTITY map1.png SYSTEM
    "http://www.anysite.net/map1.png"
    NDATA png>
```

Since the DTD has established all necessary information, the document can now create an instance of element map:

```
<map image="map1.png" />
```

Most web browsers could deal with standard png images without this elaborate setup. However, an author could apply this approach to any binary file for which a program file is available for processing.

Entities

In general, an entity is a name that the author associates with a text string by using an ENTITY definition. In the example of the previous section, the entity names an attribute value that contains a file locator and a name for the program that should process it. Chapter 1 describes predefined entities for the <, >, and & characters so that they can appear as themselves rather than as markup symbols. However, an entity can name any text that the author wishes to access elsewhere in the document.

By naming text in an ENTITY definition, the author can use the name instead of the text wherever the text should appear. This avoids frequent typing of complicated text. One advantage of this approach is that, should the author wish to change the text, it is necessary to change only the ENTITY definition. The parser will properly update all uses of the entity's name. As a further example, having provided the definition:

```
<!ENTITY MH "McGraw-Hill">
```

the author can simply use the reference &MH; wherever the text is desired; and let the parser expand it to the string "McGraw-Hill".

You Need to Know

An entity is nothing more than a name for a text string.

XML Content Models

The actual content that makes up an element or attribute follows a *content model,* which uses a form of symbol shorthand to describe the structure of the data within the tag itself. The easiest way to grasp this is to view some examples of common element types and then break them down into what they are describing.

Table 2-4 shows the symbols used most commonly in content models. Table 2-5 lists the occurrence indicators used in content models. Table 2-2 provided some examples of their use.

Table 2-4 Symbols Used in Content Models

Symbol	Description
,	Indicates a sequence
|	Indicates an alternation
( )	Indicates a grouping

Table 2-5 Occurrence Indicators

Symbol	Description
[nothing]	Element occurs once
?	Element is optional and can occur once if used
+	Element can occur one or more times
*	Element can occur zero or more times

If #PCDATA appears in a content model, it must appear first and only once. In addition, the only allowable occurrence indicator on #PCDATA (besides no occurrence indicator) is *. In addition, the other content model options are:

- #REQUIRED. Must be present; return an error if empty.
- #IMPLIED. Optional; may be ignored if no value.
- #FIXED value. Every instance of that element must have the value specified.
- EMPTY. Contains only markup without data.

Below is a list of example element definitions with explanations:

- <!ELEMENT a (b+)> describes an element named a with a child element b that appears one or more times.
- <!ELEMENT b EMPTY> describes an element named b as an EMPTY element.
- <!ELEMENT a (b,c)> describes an element named a with b and c elements that each appear once and in this order.
- <!ELEMENT a (b|c)*> describes an element named a with a b or c element that appears as many times as needed.

- `<!ELEMENT a (#PCDATA |b|c) *>` describes an element named a with either a `PCDATA` component, a b element, or a c element that can appear as many times as needed.
- `>!ELEMENT a (b, (c|d)*)>` describes an element named with a b element that appears once and then a c or d element that can appear as many times as needed.
- `<!ELEMENT a (b?, (c|d)+)>` describes an element named a with an optional b element and then a c or d element that can appear one or more times.
- `<!ELEMENT a (b?,(c+|d+))>` describes an element named a with an optional b element and then a c or d element that can appear one or more times each.

Element Structure

Before moving forward with the motion picture example, recall the following key elements:

```
title
year
genre
director
cast
music
```

Although an author's choice of when to use elements versus attributes could be somewhat arbitrary, it is easier to search based on elements than based on attributes. The quantities that follow might serve well as attributes because they are nonessential, and it is less likely that there will be searches based on the information they contain:

```
certification
runtime
country
language
medium
```

Before making the element structure final, decide whether to create a small number of elements with a lot of attributes each or a large num-

Table 2-6 Elements and Attributes for the Motion Picture Example

Element	Possible Attributes
`<!ELEMENT title (#PCDATA)>`	`language, alternate title, country, certification, runtime`
`<!ELEMENT year (#PCDATA)>`	`academy_awards, distributor`
`<!ELEMENT genre (#PCDATA)>`	`category, medium`
`<!ELEMENT director (#PCDATA)>`	`director_of_photography, cinematographer, Editor`

ber of elements with fewer attributes each. The general approach here is to compromise on that issue. Returning to the issue of elements versus attributes, a simple rule to use when the choice is not otherwise obvious is to make more permanent items elements and less permanent items attributes. Table 2-6 lists one choice of elements and their associated attributes for the motion picture element.

Remember

In a DTD, one should define data as an ELEMENT if it corresponds to essential or time-fixed information or if there is a strong likelihood that there will be a search based on the information that it contains. Otherwise, an ATTRIBUTE might be more appropriate.

Attribute Structure

The attribute structure allows one to qualify an element and further refine or define the data it conveys. However, attributes are not mandatory.
Consider a simple DTD declaration:

```
<!ELEMENT title (#PCDATA)>
<!ATTLIST title alternate_title CDATA #IMPLIED>
```

If the first DTD line were the only line, then one would create a title entity in the document by simply enclosing some text in the proper tags:

```
<title> Joe Jacoby </title>
```

Because the second DTD line defines an optional (#IMPLIED) attribute, this document definition is still valid, even with the attribute definition. However, the attribute definition in the second DTD line makes the following data also valid:

```
<title> Joe Jacoby
   alternate_title="The life of Joe Jacoby"
</title>
```

One can use multiple ATTLIST statements to declare multiple attributes for the same element. The following is a complete DTD definition for entity title:

```
<!ELEMENT title (#PCDATA)>
<!ATTLIST title language CDATA #IMPLIED>
<!ATTLTST title alternate_title CDATA #IMPLIED>
<!ATTLIST title country CDATA #IMPLIED>
<!ATTLIST title certification CDATA #IMPLIED>
<!ATTLIST title runtime #IMPLIED>
```

The following is a complete DTD definition for entity motionpicture:

```
<!ELEMENT motionpicture(title, year, genre,
   director)>
```

```
<!ELEMENT title (#PCDATA)>
<!ATTLIST title language CDATA #IMPLIED>
<!ATTLIST title alternate_title CDATA #IMPLIED>
<!ATTLIST title country CDATA #IMPLIED>
<!ATTLIST title certification #IMPLIED>
<!ATTLIST title runtime #IMPLIED>

<!ELEMENT year (#PCDATA)>
<!ATTLIST year academy_awards CDATA #IMPLIED>
<!ATTLIST year distributor CDATA #IMPLIED>

<!ELEMENT genre (#PCDATA)>
<!ATTLIST genre category CDATA #IMPLIED>
<!ATTLIST genre medium CDATA #IMPLIED>

<!ELEMENT director (#PCDATA)>
<!ATTLIST director director_of_photography
   CDATA> #IMPLIED>
<!ATTLIST director cinematographer
   CDATA #IMPLIED>
<!ATTLIST director editor CDATA #IMPLIED>
```

 **Note!**

Here are a few other simple points to keep in mind when deciding whether to use elements or attributes:

a. Too many attributes can make a document hard to read.
b. Attributes alone cannot describe the document structure; elements are also necessary,
c. Attributes are best for simple information; for more complex information, an element is better.

Review Questions

Review Question 2.1 If the prologue (the opening line and processing instructions) of the XML document states `standalone="no"`, how is the location of the DTD indicated?
Answer: In standard URI syntax, either as a local path or fully qualified URI.

Review Question 2.2 Can there be more than one DTD per XML document?
Answer: Yes, there can be multiples as long as namespace conventions are observed.

Review Question 2.3 What is the foundation of the XML document?
Answer: The element.

Review Question 2.4 What are some differences between an element and an attribute?
Answer: Elements provide the basic building blocks of the document; attributes further describe elements.

Review Question 2.5 Is a DTD required for a document to be validated?
Answer: Yes, it is required for validation.

Review Question 2.6 What is meant by an in-line DTD?
Answer: The elements are declared within the XML document.

Review Question 2.7 A DTD is required for an XML document to be:
    a. Valid
    b. Well-formed
    c. Parsed
    d. All of the above
Answer: a

Review Question 2.8 How is a DTD shared between XML documents?
Answer: By referencing the address in the processing instructions.

Review Question 2.9 Name two types of industries or academic disciplines where a common DTD is available.

Answer: Examples: academics, aerospace, automotive, computers and electronics, financial services, health care, insurance, petrochemicals, retail, telecommunications, and utilities/energy.

Review Question 2.10 Can one edit a DTD?
Answer: Yes, just like any other document.

Review Question 2.11 Binary data is not parsed. True or false?
Answer: True

Review Question 2.12 What type of tag identifies a helper application?
Answer: NOTATION

Review Question 2.13 What is the purpose and use of each of the following symbols in a DTD?
  a. *
  b. ,
  c. ?
  d. |
Answer: * is a wildcard meaning one, many, or none; , separates list items; ? means one or none; and | means alternation (or).

Review Question 2.14 Is an attribute mandatory?
Answer: Only if it is #REQUIRED.

Review Question 2.15 What symbol indicates an optional attribute?
Answer: #IMPLIED

Solved Problems

Create a DTD and an XML document for a simple music collection.

Solved Problem 2.1 Define the elements and attributes that will describe information in the collection.
Solution: The elements will be title, song, artist, and composer. The attributes will be genre, year, and length.

Solved Problem 2.2 Create a DTD (in-line).
Solution: Here is a suggested DTD and the element order:

```
<!ELEMENT CD (title, artist+, song*)>
<!ELEMENT title (#PCDATA)>
<!ELEMENT artist ((firstname*, lastname) |
  group?)>
<!ELEMENT firstname (#PCDATA)>
<!ELEMENT lastname (#PCDATA)>
<!ELEMENT group (#PCDATA)>
<!ELEMENT song (#PCDATA)>
<!ATTLIST song genre CDATA #IMPLIED>
<!ATTLIST song year CDATA #IMPLIED>
<!ATTLIST song length CDATA #IMPLIED>
```

Solved Problem 2.3 Create the prologue for the document.
Solution: `<?xml version="1.0" standalone=`
`"yes" encoding="UTF-8"?>`

Solved Problem 2.4 Create a well-formed XML document.
Solution: An XML document using the in-line DTD:

```
<?xml version="1.0" standalone="yes"
encoding="UTF-8"?>
<!DOCTYPE title [
<!ELEMENT cd (title, artist+, song*)>
<!ELEMENT title #PCDATA)>
<!ELEMENT artist (firstname*, lastname)
 group?)>
<!ELEMENT firstname (#PCDATA)>
<!ELEMENT lastname (#PCDATA)>
<!ELEMENT group (#PCDATA)>
<!ELEMENT song (#PCDATA)>
<!ATTLIST song genre CDATA #IMPLIED>
<!ATTLIST song year CDATA #IMPLIED>
<!ATTLIST song length CDATA #IMPLIED>
]>
<cd>
<title>Beautiful Maladies</title>
<artist>
<firstname>Tom</firstname>
<lastname>Waits</lastname>
```

```
</artist>
<song genre="folk" year="1987"
 length="2:42">
 Hang on St. Christopher</song>
<Song genre="urban folk" year="1987"
length="3:51">
Temptation</song>
<song genre="urban folk" year="1985"
length="3:45 ">
 Clap Hands</song>
</cd>
```

Chapter 3
SCHEMA

✔ *Schema Concepts*
✔ *Schema for Structures*
✔ *Schema for Datatypes*

Schema Concepts

Document Type Definitions (DTDs), the common validation tools for XML document models, have been around since the promulgation of Standard Generalized Markup Language (SGML). Although DTDs have several advantages, long-term usage by XML professionals being one of them, there are also several disadvantages:

- They follow a different syntax than XML.
- They lack detailed datatyping.
- Declarations are difficult to read and understand.

The World Wide Web Consortium (W3C) proposed the XML Schema Language as an alternative to the DTD. Although XML Schema is a more complex language, it allows the document author to define strict datatypes for both element and attribute values.

The basic concepts that underlie XML Schema are similar to those for XML DTDs, and the main purpose is the same: validation. For example, consider an

44

online educational company's enrollment progress report. It collects data class by class. An XML Schema defines a strict hierarchy and datatypes for the data and therefore enforces document structure and data integrity. The following is an example of an XML document using enrollment data:

```
<?xml version="1.0"?>
 <enrollment
   xmlns=
   "http://www.lanw.com/namespaces/enrollment">
   <class>
   <title>XHTML Part I/title>
   <period name="Session 1">125</period>
   <period name="Session 2">67</period>
   <period name="Session 3">115</period>
   </class>
 <class>
   <title>XHTML Part II/title>
   <Period name="Session 1">110</period>
   <Period name="Session 2">89</period>
   <Period name="Session 3">122</period>
   </class>
 <class>
   <title>XHTML Part III</title>
   <Period name="Session 1">87</period>
   <Period name="Session 2>44</period>
   <Period name="Session 3>77</period>
   </class>
 <class>
   <title>An Introduction to XML</title>
   <Period name="Session 1">101</period>
   <Period name="Session 2">88</period>
   <Period name="Session 3">112</period>
   </class>
 <class>
   <title>Transforming XML with XSLT</title>
   <Period name="Session 1">90</period>
   <Period name="Session 2">69</Period>
   <Period name="Session 3">102</period>
   </class>
```

```
<class>
  <title>XML Content Management and Delivery
  </title>
  <Period name="Session 1">67</period>
  <Period name="Session 2">55</period>
  <Period name="Session 3">82</period>
  </class>
 </enrollment>
```

The following could serve as an XML Schema to validate the document:

```
<schema
 xmlns="http://www.w3.org/2001/XMLSchema"
 xmlns:enr="http://www.lanw.com/namespaces/
  enrollment"
 targetNamespace=
  "http://www.lanw.com/namespaces/enrollment">
<element name="enrollment">
 <complexType>
   <element ref="enr:class" minOccurs="1"
   maxOccurs="unbounded"/>
 </complexType>
</element>
<element name="class">
 <complexType>
   <sequence>
    <element ref="enr:title"/>
    <element ref="enr:period" minOccurs="1"
    maxOccurs="unbounded"/>
   </sequence>
 </complexType>
</element>
<element name="title" type="string"/>
<element name="period" type="string"/>
 <complexType>
   <attribute name="name" type="string"
   use="default" value="unknown"/>
 </complexType>
</element>
</schema>
```

Note the use of `minOccurs` and `maxOccurs` to specify how many times an element must be present. Another innovation is the use of a ref to specify where the parser can find the element's definition. For example,

```
<element ref="enr:title"/>
```

specifies an element whose definition is the same as that of element `title` in the namespace with local name `enr`.

Observe that the schema is itself a well-formed document. One of the advantages to using XML Schema is that it follows XML syntax rules, and an XML parser can verify it.

Remember

The syntax rules of XML are:

a. Elements and attributes are case-sensitive.
b. All nonempty elements must have an opening and closing tag.
c. All attributes must have values, and those values must be in quotation marks.
d. All elements require termination as in: `<empty/>`.
e. All elements must nest correctly.

Since DTDs existed long before namespaces, they do not support them. By contrast, the definition of W3C XML Schema elements reside in a namespace at http://www.w3.org/2001/XMLSchema, and schema authors use namespaces extensively. It is possible to use the above namespace as a default or to define it with an `xsd` prefix and to precede all schema elements with it. For example to use the schema element tag, one would employ syntax like the following:

```
<xsd:element> . . . </xsd:element:>.
```

The XML Schema can establish a namespace to store its declared elements and attributes. The `targetNamespace` attribute provides the means of accomplishing this. The schema in the following example will store its element and attribute definitions at the site `http://www.lanw.com/namespace/store`:

```
<schema
 xmlns="http://www.w3.org/2001/XMLSchema"
 xmlns:enr=
 "http://www.lanw.com/namespaces/enrollment"
 targetNamespace=
 "http://www.lanw.com/namespaces/store">
<element name="enrollment">
 <complexType>
  <element ref="enr:class" minOccurs="1"
  maxOccurs="unbounded"/>
 </complexType>
</element>
</schema>
```

You Need to Know ✔

With one exception, every `xmlns` attribute definition must provide an associated name (such as `enr` in `xmlns:enr`) for the namespace it specifies. The one exception is the *default namespace*. Use of an item in a named namespace requires a corresponding name prefix (as in `ref="enr:class"`). All items in the default namespace are automatically defined and visible in the document without the need for a `ref` attribute.

A schema permits the definition of *complex types*, data types that contain multiple components. The following complex-type definition uses a sequence structure to require that firstname always precedes lastname:

```
<complexType name="fullnameType">
 <sequence>
  <element name="firstName" type="string"/>
  <element name="lastName" type="string"/>
 </sequence>
complexType>
```

It is possible to use this complex-type definition to declare elements of this type in other locations. For example, one can create an element named customer that must follow the fullnameType definition. (In other words, it must always have firstName and lastName child elements in order). Here is an example:

```
<element name="customer" type="fullnameType"/>
```

The second way to declare complex types is to define them without a name as a part of another declaration. In this case, since the item is anonymous (has no name), it will not be possible to later reference this definition to declare elements of the same type:

```
<element name="customer">
 <complexType>
  <sequence>
   <element name="firstName" type="string"/>
   <element name="lastName" type="string"/>
  </sequence>
 </complexType>
</element>
```

Schema for Structures

 **Note!**

The following discussion of schemas structures involves frequent use of the following adjectives:
Local. Qualifies an element or attribute whose definition takes place within the definition of another element of the schema.
Global. Qualifies an element or attribute whose definition takes place directly within the `schema` element definition, but not within the definition of any other element.

The W3C *XML Schema Part 1: Structures* document defines the schema vocabulary. Because the XML Schema standard is an XML vocabulary, it uses elements and attributes. The following sections cover the use of many of the XML Schema elements and attributes defined by the structures document.

One could use the following DTD syntax to declare a `song` element with three child elements: `title`, `artist`, and `fileSize`.

```
<!ELEMENT song (title, artist, fileSize)>
<!ELEMENT title (#PCDATA)>
<!ELEMENT artist (#PCDATA)>
<!ELEMENT fileSize (#PCDATA)>
```

Now, consider the schema equivalent:

```
<schema
 xmlns=
 "http://www.w3.org/2001/XMLSchema"
 xmlns:song=
 "http://www.lanw.com/namespaces/song"
```

```
targetNamespace=
"http://www.lanw.com/namespaces/song">
<element name="song">
 <complexType>
  <sequence>
   <element ref="song:title"/>
   <element ref="song:artist"/>
   <element ref="song:fileSize"/>
  </sequence>
 </complexType>
</element>
<element name="title" type="string"/>
<element name="artist" type="string"/>
<element name="fileSize" type="string"/>
</schema>
```

Notice that schema is the root element (also known as the *document element*). It requires a namespace declaration that points to the schema namespace. In this example, it is the default namespace; therefore, it does not need the xsd prefix. This means that all elements that do not use a prefix belong to the schema namespace.

In addition, there is also a namespace for song elements, which will have the prefix song:. This enables references to elements that are declared elsewhere.

The third and final defined namespace is known as the *target namespace*, defining the namespace of elements that the schema can validate.

As with the DTD example, the schema document has four element type declarations. The first declaration is as follows:

```
<element name="song">
 <complexType>
  <sequence>
   <element ref="song:title"/>
   <element ref="song:artist"/>
   <element ref="song:fileSize"/>
  </sequence>
 </complexType>
</element>
```

The `element` element (yes, that's right) declares an element. The name attribute names the element. In this case, the element has the name `song`. The next step is to identify the element as a `complexType` because it contains other elements.

XML Schema permits the definition of several different types of content models, all using different schema elements and attributes. For example, most of the following schema elements (also called *compositors*) can translate to DTD equivalents:

- `all`. No DTD equivalent.
- `any`. Similar to the DTD `ANY` keyword.
- `choice`. Similar to the DTD pipe bar (|) connector.
- `group`. No DTD equivalent.
- `sequence`. Similar to the DTD comma (,) connector.

There are a few schema attributes that serve to define content models as well:

- `minOccurs="value"`. Similar to the DTD occurrence indicators (?,+, and *) .
- `maxOccurs="value"`. Similar to the DTD occurrence indicators (?,+, and *) .

The sequence element defines an ordered sequence for allowable child elements. For example, the following snippet requires that the child elements appear in order of `title`, `artist`, and `fileSize`:

```
<sequence>
 <element ref="song:title"/>
 <element ref=song.artist"/>
 <element ref=song:fileSize"/>
</sequence>
```

There are two ways to use the `element` element: as a definition and as a reference. This example uses references as indicated by `ref=`.

Now, what about that `song` prefix? Well, having declared an element within the scope of a `targetName` space, it is necessary to reference it as part of that space by using the proper prefix.

Take a second to look at the `namespace` definitions:

```
<schema
 xmlns=
 "http://www.w3.org/2001/XMLSchema"
 xmlns:song=
 "http://www.lanw.com/namespaces/song"
 targetNamespace=
 "http://www.lanw.com/namespaces/song">
```

Since the first namespace has no name, it is the default for this schema document. This means that if one uses (or references) any non-schema elements, each must have an alternative prefix. The last two namespaces work together. The last one (targetNamespace) defines a namespace for association with all declared elements. This is not an xmlns namespace definition; this simply states that if a document uses these elements, it must reference the namespace that resides at the indicated URI. The second namespace (xmlns:song) is present specifically to make that possible by providing an appropriate prefix through which to access the URI.

Remember

If the default namespace for a schema entity is not its target-Namespace, then one must define an xmlns namespace for the tar-getNamespace URI and use it as a prefix when referring to any element or attribute defined in the schema element.

The following example is identical to the preceding complete schema example except that, instead of using a sequence element to require first a title, then an artist, and then a fileSize, it uses a choice element to require a choice of exactly one of them

```
<schema
 xmlns=
 "http://www.w3.org/2001/XMLSchema"
 xmlns:song=
 "http://www.lanw.com/namespaces/song"
 targetNamespace=
 "http://www.lanw.com/namespaces/song">
 <element name="song">
  <complexType>
   <choice>
    <element ref="song:title"/>
    <element ref="song:artist"/>
    <element ref="song:fileSize"/>
   </choice>
  </complexType>
 </element>
 <element name="title" type="string"/>
 <element name="artist" type="string"/>
 <element name="fileSize" type="string"/>
</schema>
```

Addition of minOccurs and maxOccurs modifies the song element to permit one or more choices of the three types of child elements:

```
<schema
 xmlns=
 "http://www.w3.org/2001/XMLSchema"
 xmlns:song=
 "http://www.lanw.com/namespaces/song"
 targetNamespace=
 "http://www.lanw.com/namespaces/song">
 <element name="song">
  <complexType>
  <choiceminOccurs="1" maxOccurs="unbounded">
   <element ref="song:title"/>
   <element ref="song:artist"/>
   <element ref="song:fileSize"/>
  </choice>
  </complexType>
```

```
  </element>
  <element name="title" type="string"/>
  <element name="artist" type="string"/>
  <element name="fileSize" type="string"/>
</schema>
```

The following version uses an all element to require all three children exactly once, but to impose no restrictions on the order in which they appear:

```
<schema
  xmlns=
  "http://www.w3.org/2001/XMLSchema"
  xmlns:song=
  "http://www.lanw.com/namespaces/song"
  targetNamespace=
  "http://www.lanw.com/namespaces/song">
  <element name="song">
   <complexType>
   <all minOccurs="1" maxOccurs="unbounded">
    <element ref="song:title"/>
    <element ref="song:artist"/>
    <element ref="song:fileSize"/>
   </all>
   </complexType>
  </element>
  <element name="title" type="string"/>
  <element name="artist" type="string"/>
  <element name="fileSize" type="string"/>
</schema>
```

Declaring attributes is much like declaring elements. For attribute declarations, one uses the attribute element. Suppose that the goal is to add a genre attribute to the song element. The DTD syntax would be as follows:

```
<!ELEMENT song (title, artist, fileSize)>
<!ATTLIST song genre CDATA #REQUIRED>
```

Now take a look at the XML Schema equivalent:

```
<schema
 xmlns=
 "http://www.w3.org/2001/XMLSchema"
 xmlns:song=
 "http://www.lanw.com/namespaces/song"
 targetNamespace=
 "http://www.lanw.com/namespaces/song">
 <element name="song">
  <complexType>
   <sequence>
    <element ref="song:title"/>
    <element ref="song:artist"/>
    <element ref="song:fileSize"/>
   </sequence>
   <attribute name="genre" type="string"
   use="required"/>
  </complexType>
 </element>
 <element name="title" type="string"/>
 <element name="artist" type="string"/>
 <element name="fileSize" type="string"/>
</schema>
```

This example defines the genre attribute, which is required and can take any character data as its value. The most common attributes used with the attribute element are:

- name="name". This defines the name for the attribute.
- ref="name". This references global attribute declarations. Global declarations are elements or attributes defined as children of the schema element and referenced later. Note that global declarations cannot contain references.
- type="name". This defines the datatype for the attribute.
- use="Prohibited |optional |required |default |fixed". This serves to indicate whether the attribute is required or optional. One may also declare the attribute to contain a fixed or default value. In this case one must define the fixed or default value with the value attribute. The default value is optional.

- `value="string"`. This defines the fixed or `default` value, when appropriate as determined by the `use` value.

The following example defines an attribute with a default value:

```
<schema
 xmlns=
 "http://www.w3.org/2001/XMLSchema"
 xmlns:song=
 "http://www.lanw.com/namespaces/song"
 targetNamespace=
 "http://www.lanw.com/namespaces/song">
 <element name="song">
  <complexType>
    <sequence>
     <element ref="song:title"/>
     <element ref="song:artist"/>
     <element ref="song:fileSize"/>
    </sequence>
   <attribute name="genre" type="string"
   use="default" value="unknown"/>
  </complexType>
 </element>
 <element name="title" type="string"/>
 <element name="artist" type="string"/>
 <element name="fileSize" type="string"/>
</schema>
```

The next example creates a new attribute that will identify the URI where the song is available for downloading:

```
<schema
 xmlns=
 "http://www.w3.org/2001/XMLSchema"
 xmlns:song=
 "http://www.lanw.com/namespaces/song"
 targetNamespace=
 "http://www.lanw.com/namespaces/song">
 <element name="song">
  <complexType>
    <sequence>
```

```
    <element ref="song:title"/>
    <element ref="song:artist"/>
    <element ref="song:fileSize"/>
  </sequence>
  <attribute name="genre" type="string"
  use="default" value="unknown"/>
  <attribute name="href" type="uriReference"
  use="required"/>
  </complexType>
 </element>
<element name="title" type="string"/>
<element name="artist" type="string"/>
<element name="fileSize" type="string"/>
</schema>
```

The new addition is a required attribute named href that can accept a uriReference datatype. The uriReference and string datatypes are the only two datatypes discussed here; however, there are several to choose from, and authors can create new ones, as discussed in the following section.

Don't Forget!

The word "element" has many levels of meaning in a schema:

  a. The schema itself is an element of type schema.
  b. The schema is the root element of its own XML document
  b. A schema element defines user elements and user attributes using elements from the schema namespace that have familiar names like: element, attribute, sequence, choice, etc.

Schema for Datatypes

One of the main drawbacks to using DTDs is that they do not allow for sophisticated datatyping. Take a second to refresh your memory:

- *DTD Attribute datatypes:* ID, IDREF(S), CDATA, NOTA-TION, ENTITY, ENTITIES, NMTOKEN(S), and enumerated values
- *DTD Element datatypes:* PCDATA and/or child elements

These are the only available datatypes with DTDs! One of the reasons schemas have become so attractive is that they allow for more sophisticated datatyping. Wouldn't it be nice to require the ISBN number to contain exactly 10 digits? When it comes time to validate the documents, there are no entry mistakes. What about dates? Would it be helpful to define a naming convention for dates? XML Schema datatyping is defined by the *XML Schema Part 2: Datatypes* document. Take a second to look at a DTD fragment:

```
<!ATTLIST book price CDATA #IMPLIED>
```

With this declaration, a document author is free to use any character data string as the value; for example, the following data would validate, despite its obvious shortcomings:

```
<book price="silly">
<book price="22">
<book price=".">
```

With XML Schema, however, one can define the value as having type decimal. For example:

```
<attribute name="price" type="decimal"/>
```

Therefore, only a decimal number such as the following would be acceptable:

```
<book price="22.22">
```

The schema specification organizes the datatypes using several different distinctions:

- *Primitive versus derived.* Derived datatypes are defined in terms of other datatypes. Primitive datatypes are not.
- *Atomic versus list versus union.* Atomic datatypes are those with values that the specification regards as being indivisible. List datatypes are defined as those with values that consist of a finite-length sequence of values of an atomic datatype. Finally, union datatypes are those in which value spaces and lexical spaces are the union of the value spaces and lexical spaces of two or more datatypes.
- *Built-in versus user-derived.* Built-in datatypes are those that the specification defines (they can be derived or primitive). Schema designers (like you) create user-derived datatypes.

For more information on datatypes, see the XML Schema Datatype specification (www.w3.org/TR/xmlschema-2/).

There are two different types of built-in datatypes: primitive and derived. Primitive datatypes are the foundation for all other datatypes. Derived datatypes are based on (built from) the primitive datatypes. Table 3-1 defines all primitive datatypes.

The following are the derived datatypes defined by the datatypes document:

```
normalizedString
token
language
ID
IDREF
IDREFS
ENTITY
ENTITIES
NMTOKEN
NMTOKENS
Name
NCName
integer
nonPositiveInteger
```

Table 3-1 XML Schema Primitive Datatypes

Datatype	Example(Value (s)
string	Hello World
boolean	{true, false}
float	12.56E3, 12, 12560, 0, -0, INF, -INF,NAN
double	12.56E3, 12, 12560, 0, -0, INF, -INF,NAN
decimal	7.08
duration	P0Y1347M
dateTime	1999-05-31T13:20:00-05:00
time	13:20:00-05:00
date	2001-07-29
gYearMonth	2001-07
gYear	2001
gDay	29
gMonthDay	07-29
gmonth	07
hexBinary	0Fb7
base64Binary	bW9t
anyURI	http:/www.lanw.com
Qname	mc:song
NOTATION	notation

negativeInteger
long
int
short
byte
nonNegativeInteger
unsignedLong
unsignedInt
unsignedShort
unsignedByte
positiveInteger

Review Questions

Review Question 3.1 XML Schema was created by the W3C as an alternative for which of the following?
- a. RELAX
- b. Schematron
- c. DTD
- d. XDR

Answer: c. XML Schema was created as an alternative for XML 1.0 DTDs.

Review Question 3.2 Which of the following is not true about XML Schema?
- a. It allows users to define patterns for their own datatypes.
- b. It is namespace aware.
- c. It allows for complex datatyping.
- d. It is defined in one specification document.

Answer: d. XML Schema is defined by two specification documents: *XML Schema Part 1: Structures* and *XML Schema Part 2: Datatypes*.

Review Question 3.3 XML Schema defines an equivalent for DTD general entities.
- a. True
- b. False

Answer: b. False. XML Schema does not define equivalents for DTD general entities.

Review Question 3.4 Which of the following is a complete element declaration?
- a. `<element name="contact" type="string">`
- b. `<element name="contact">`
- c. `<element type="string" name="contact"/>`
- d. `<element type="string">`

Answer: c. The following complete element declaration allows for a `contact` element that can only contain a string datatype:
```
<element type="string" name="contact"/>
```

Review Question 3.5 Which of the following is an incomplete attribute declaration?

a. `<attribute name="isbn" type="isbnType"/>`
b. `<attribute name="isbn" type="integer"/>`
c. `<attribute ref="contactID"/>`
d. `<attribute name="contactID"/>`

Answer: d. Attribute declarations can reference either predefined attribute declarations or both the name and type must be defined.

Review Question 3.6 Which of the following attribute combinations in the element declarations requires that the contact element occurs at least once and may repeat five times?

a. `<element name="contact" type="string" minOccurs="1" maxOccurs="5"/>`
b. `<element name="contact" type="string" minOccurs="1" maxOccurs="5"/>`
c. `<element name="contact" type="string" maxOccurs="1" minOccurs="5"/>`
d. `<element name="contact" type="string" maxOccurs="5"/>`

Answer: a. The `maxOccurs` attribute defines the maximum number of occurrences, whereas the `minOccurs` attribute defines the minimum number of occurrences for an element.

Review Question 3.7 Of the following, which is not a category of datatype defined by XML Schema?

a. Derived
b. Combined
c. Primitive
d. Atomic

Answer: b. Derived, primitive, and atomic are types of datatypes defined by the XML Schema specification.

Review Question 3.8 Which of the following does not use the string datatype properly?

a. `<element name="name" type="string"/>`
b. `<attribute name="name" type="string"/>`
c. `<complexType name="name" type="string"/>`
d. `<restriction base="string">`

Answer: c. The `complexType` element cannot contain a type attribute that is used to define a datatype.

Review Question 3.9 Which of the following is a correct usage of the `dateTime` datatype?

 a. `1999-05-31Tl3:20:00-05:00`
 b. `1999-T05-31-13:20:00-05:00`
 c. `1999-31TI3:20:00-05:00`
 d. `1999-05-31TI3:20:00`

Answer: a. `1999-05-31T13:20:00-05:00` is the correct use of the `dateTime` datatype.:

Review Question 3.10 Which of the following is not a primitive datatype?

 a. `integer`
 b. `duration`
 c. `gYear`
 d. `boolean`

Answer: a. `integer` is a derived datatype.

Solved Problems

Solved Problem 3.1 Define a declaration for a `contact` element that contains `name` and `email` children elements. The `name` and `email` elements must occur only once and must occur in the order of `name` followed by `email`.
Solution:

```
<element name="contact">
 <complexType>
  <sequence>
   <element name="name" type="string"/>
   <element name="email" type="string"/>
  </sequence>
 </complexType>
</element>
```

Solved Problem 3.2 Add an attribute declaration to the contact element. The attribute should be an `ID` datatype with the name `id`.
Solution:

```
<element name="contact">
 <complexType>
  <sequence>
```

```
  <element name="name" type="string"/>
  <element name="email" type="string"/>
 </sequence>
 <attribute name="id" type="ID"/>
 </complexType>
</element>
```

Solved Problem 3.3 Declare a complexType definition with the name contactType that allows for the same content model as the contact element in Problem 3.1.

Solution:

```
<complexType name="contactType">
 <sequence>
  <element name="name" type="string"/>
  <element name="email" type="string"/>
 </sequence>
</complexType>
```

Solved Problem 3.4 Define an attribute declaration that references the contactType definition. Name the new element customer.

Solution:

```
<element name="customer"
ref="contactType">
```

Solved Problem 3.5 Create an attribute declaration that would be the equivalent to the following DTD attribute list declaration:<!ATTLIST book cat NMTOKENS #REQUIRED>. Do not define the accompanying book element declaration, only the attribute declaration.

Solution:

```
<attribute name="cat" type="NMTOKENS"
  use="required"/>
```

Chapter 4
CASCADING
STYLE SHEETS

IN THIS CHAPTER:

- ✔ *CSS in Browsers and Components*
- ✔ *The* `display: block` *Property*
- ✔ *Fonts*
- ✔ *Text Alignment*
- ✔ *Borders*
- ✔ *Backgrounds*
- ✔ *Real-World Issues: Using CSS for XML Delivery*

CSS in Browsers and Components

Cascading Style Sheets (CSS) allow the XML author to present a document in an attractive fashion and inform the browser (or other user agent) of the style properties to be applied to components of the XML document. The tags used in XML, although they may appear to be very much like HTML tags, offer no indication of intended presentation markup. Remember that XML is *content-driven* as opposed to *presentation-driven*. Through the use of

a CSS style sheet, one can specify the presentation format for the XML document.

This book focuses on the CSS2 standard, but CSS3 is already in the works. The complete CSS2 specification (and any updates) are available at http://www.w3.org/TR/CSS2/.

The main players in the browser market are Microsoft Internet Explorer 6+, Netscape Navigator 7+, and Safari (Macintosh only). In addition, there are two other browsers that are of particular interest for their strong XML and CSS support: Opera 5 and the Amaya browser. Browsers offer a mixed and varied bag of native XML support, but by incorporating CSS, they all have a greater success in presenting XML. Browsers will most likely continue to evolve *toward* the specifications as opposed to *away* from them, and the examples presented here focus on the current crop of user agents.

A CSS style sheet provides additional (and, in the case of XML, all) presentation information for the documents to which it is applied. This information depends upon the elements or class of elements used in the content of the document. Most of the CSS concepts apply to HTML and the XHTML as well as to XML.

Here are a few of the basic terms from the W3C standard:

- *Style sheet.* A style sheet consists of additional markup in the form of statements that govern *presentation* of the document. Style sheets generally are one of three basic types (which provide the cascade): *author, user,* or *user agent.* The first of these, the *author* style, is presentation specified by the author of the document or the software used to create the document. This style is subordinate to the *user* style, which is the style the user has personally set, usually through browser preferences. Finally, there is the style dictated by the *user agent,* which is the style sheet that typically takes precedence over the preceding two types of style markup and often is a limitation brought about by the browser or another user agent. In practice, the document author provides values for each attribute, allowing them to *cascade* down to the defaults of the browser or software.
- *Valid style sheet.* Like XML itself, CSS should validate to the accepted standards indicated for the level of CSS used. Luckily, any CSS1 documents should validate against CSS2, but for critical applications, it is advisable to update to current standards.

As part of the validation process, the style sheet undergoes checks for conformity to rules, property names, and property values defined in the CSS specification.

- *Source document.* The *source document* is the document to which one or more style sheets refer. This is encoded in a language that represents the document as a tree of elements. Each element consists of a name that identifies the type of element and, optionally, a number of attributes.

- *Document language.* This is the encoding language used in the source document, for example, XML, XHTML, or HTML.

- *Element.* This is the familiar element as used in SGML, XML, HTML, and XHTML. It is the primary syntactic construct of the document language. Many CSS style sheet rules use the names of elements such as `br`, `table`, and `ul` (from HTML) to specify rendering information for them.

- *Attribute.* This provides information on an element in the form of an attribute-value pair. The value must be quoted. Single or double quotes are both acceptable.

- *Content.* This is the content associated with an element in the source document; not all elements have content, in which case they are *empty elements.* The content of an element may include text. In addition, it can include a number of *subelements,* in which case the element is called the *parent* of those *subelements.*

- *Rendered content.* This is the content of an element after the application of the rendering of the CSS style sheets. Rendered content also may be alternate text for an element (for example, the value of the HTML `alt` attribute) and may include items inserted implicitly or explicitly by the style sheet, such as bullets, numbering, and so on. The rendered content of a replaced element comes from outside the source document.

- *Document tree.* This is the tree of elements encoded in the source document. Each element in this tree has exactly one *parent,* with the exception of the root element, which has none.

- *Child.* Element A is called the *child* of element B if and only if element B is the *parent* of element A.

- *Descendant.* Element A is called a *descendant* of element B if either element A is a *child* of element B or element A is the *child* of element C that is a *descendant* of element B.

- *Ancestor.* Element A is called an *ancestor* of element B if and only if element B is a *descendant* of element A.

- *Sibling.* Element A is called a *sibling* of element B if and only if elements B and A share the same *parent* element. Element A is a *preceding sibling* if it comes *before* element B in the document tree. Element B is a *following sibling* if it comes *after* element B in the document tree.

A CSS *rule* generally consists of four parts: selectors, declarations, properties, and values. A *selector* is any element that one uses to select where the style should apply, for example p (in HTML). A *declaration* is the style itself, (e.g., color: green). The declaration has two parts: the *property* (color) and the *value* (green). Notice that the syntax is slightly different from that of an attribute-value pair in HTML. In CSS, the property and the value are separated with a colon, which delimits the attribute from the value. All property declarations end with a semicolon, for example:

```
p {color: green; font-family:Arial}.
```

Finally, there are two levels of declaring styles: *in-line* and *block*. In-line does *not* cause a line break when applied, whereas block inserts a leading line break. The next section discusses both in detail.

Style declarations often occur in a separate file from the source document and receive a .css extension. The XML document frequently specifies the CSS file via a processing instruction (PI) as in:

```
<?xml:stylesheet type="text/css"
href="example.css"?>
```

The same path/URI rules apply to CSS files as to DTD or other included files.

The display: block Property

The display: block property is very similar to and reminiscent of the results given by the paragraph (p) element in HTML. A *block* of text receives assignment of a style as an aggregate, with a preceding line break applied. The display: block property can contain styles of the `display: inline` variety without incurring a line break. For example, one may want to apply a font style to a block of text and then emphasize a portion of that text by setting a heavier font weight without breaking the flow of the text. For this example, use the text element for the body of text and the author element for the author's name, which is the emphasized portion. Assume that following the XML document resides in the file, *exampleCSS.xml*:

```
<?xml version ="1.0"?>
<?xml:stylesheet type="text/css"
href="example.css"?>
<text>
For the duration of the semester, we will focus
on three authors, specifically
 <author>John Steinbeck</author>,
 <author>Ernest Hemingway</author>, and
 <author>J.D. Salinger</author>.
Each of these will be discussed in turn.
</text>
```

Declare the CSS style rules in the file, *example.css*:

```
text { display: block}
author ( display: inline;
         font-weight: bold}
```

Each declaration of a style has surrounding braces. Property declarations use semicolons (;) as separators since more than one can occur in the style declaration. In addition, one can provide alternate values, separated by commas (,).

This example provides for a simple `display: block` for the data contained in the text element, with no style applied other than the line break at the beginning of the rendered text. This behaves just like a standard p element in HTML. The portion of the text contained in an author element, uses a `font-weight: bold`, with no line breaks. Figure 4-1 shows the document rendered with CSS by opening the file, *exampleCSS.xml* with a browser. As requested in the style rules, the data between the `author` tags appear without line breaks, but in boldface.

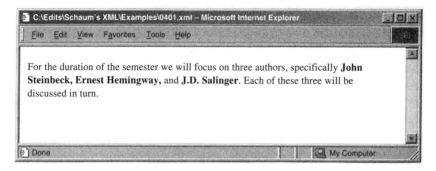

For the duration of the semester we will focus on three authors, specifically **John Steinbeck, Ernest Hemingway,** and **J.D. Salinger.** Each of these three will be discussed in turn.

Figure 4-1 XML rendered with CSS.

Don't Forget!

The blank space between `display:` and `block` in `display: block` is important. It separates property `display:` from its value, `block`.

Fonts

One of the most common uses of CSS is in rendering fonts. Because the browser is still the user agent of choice for most XML documents, the selection of font style, size, weight, and so on is of great importance to the design of the CSS document. Most of the styles that apply to fonts tend to improve one of two general aspects: design and visual appeal or readability and emphasis.

The font style *properties* are familiar to most HTML authors. CSS1 provides these basic font properties:

- `color`. Either as a color name (for example, red) or a red-green-blue (RGB) value (for example, 255, 0, 0). Since browsers may render built-in named colors differently, the use of RGB values is advisable in most circumstances.

- font-weight. Either as a keyword (bold, normal, etc.) or as a numerical value (100 through 900). For example, normal equates to 400, and bold is the same as 700.
- font-family. Use as a family name (Arial, Courier, etc.) or generic (serif, sans-serif, etc.). For cross-platform documents, use of the generic font-family grouping is the better choice because different operating systems use different names for very similar fonts. The generic groups are: serif, sans-serif, cursive, fantasy, and monospace.
- font-size. Uses one of four criteria: absolute size, relative size, length, or percentage. The absolute-size keywords are: xx-small, x-small, small, medium, large, x-large, and xx-large. Relative sizes are larger and smaller, each of which changes the absolute sizes in the direction indicated. Length and percentage values should not take the font-size table into account when calculating the font-size of the element. Negative values are not allowed.
- font-style. Selects between normal, italic, or oblique. The normal selection is an upright style, and italic and oblique refer to their respective counterparts, when available within a font family.
- text-decoration. Adds none, underline, overline, line-through, or blink.
- text-transform. Establishes case values such as capitalize, uppercase, lowercase, or none.

CSS2 adds the following font properties:

- text-shadow. Allows the creation of a shadow effect on text by specifying a shadow offset (horizontal and vertical) and optionally may specify a blur radius and a shadow color. For example:

```
h3 { text-shadow: 3px 4px 5px red }
```

This creates a red shadow offset 3 pixels to the right with 4 pixels below and a 5-pixel blur. Positive values for offset are right and below.
- font-size-adjust. Specifies a desired aspect value for a

replacement font to maintain legibility as the size of the font decreases. The larger the `font-size-adjust value`, the more legible the font will be when reduced in size.  For example, the popular font Verdana has an aspect value of 0.58; when a Verdana font size is 100 units, its x height is 58 units. For comparison, Times New Roman has an aspect value of 0.46. Verdana therefore will tend to remain more legible at smaller sizes than Times New Roman. Conversely, Verdana often will look too big if substituted for Times New Roman at a chosen size. As a result, Verdana will size slightly smaller to maintain its relative legibility.

- `font-stretch`. Selects a normal, condensed, or expanded face from a font family. An `absolute` or `relative` keyword specifies this. Absolute keyword values order from narrowest to widest: `ultra-condensed`, `extra-condensed`, `condensed`, `semi-condensed`, `normal`, `semi-expanded`, `expanded`, `extra-expanded`, and `ultra-expanded`. The relative keyword `wider` sets the value to the next expanded value above the inherited value but not increasing it above `ultra-expanded`. The relative keyword `narrower` sets the value to the next condensed value below the inherited value but not decreasing it below `ultra-condensed`.

In practice, font properties often are combined in one declaration. For example, one can modify the declaration:

```
author { display: inline;
        font-weight: bold}
```

with a font color by adding the property statement `color: green` to the declaration, which then becomes:

```
author { display: inline; font-weight: bold;
        color: green }
```

One can specify multiple properties in this way as long as they share a common element and make logical sense. As with a DTD, creating shared CSS files is a good way to ensure consistency between multiple XML documents. As always, pay close attention to the syntax, completeness, and therefore, the validity of the CSS style sheets.

Text Alignment

The `text-align` property describes how the designer intends to position, align, and justify the text within the browser window. The common values for text alignment are `left`, `right`, `center`, and `justify`. When used in conjunction with the `display: block` property, it is easy to create CSS declarations that allow the presentation to achieve the desired results. Because `text-align` inherits properties, it lends itself to use with the `div` element or other high-level text formatting elements.

Here are some examples of the use of the `text-align` property:

```
div.center { text-align: center }
div.left { text-align: left }
```

Borders

The purpose of CSS is to allow developers to enhance documents for improved readability as well as aesthetics. The `border` property has values for: `border-width`, `border-style`, and `border-color`. Each of these consists of sub-properties and attributes.

The `border-width` property is a shorthand property for setting the sub-properties `border-width-top`, `border-width-right`, `border-width-bottom`, and `border-width-left` at the same time in a style sheet. It consists of a list containing from one to four values, each of which maps to a specific aspect of the `border-width`.

The W3C specifies four forms:

- *One value*. All four border-widths receive this value. For example, all four in this example are receive the value `thin`:

  ```
  h1 { border-width: thin }
  ```

- *Two values.* Top and bottom border widths receive the first value, and right and left border widths receive the second. In the following example, the top border and bottom borders are thin and the left and right are thick:

```
hl { border-width: thin thick }
```

- *Three values.* The top border receives the first value, the right and left borders the second value, and bottom border the third value. In this example, the top border is thin, the right and left borders are thick, and the bottom is medium:

```
hl { border-width: thin thick medium }
```

- *Four values.* This sets the top, right, bottom, and left borders, respectively. In this example, the top border is thin, the right border is thick, the left border is medium, and the bottom border is thin. The acceptable values for border-width are thin, medium, thick, or a length value, as long as the value is not a negative number:

```
hl { border-width: thin thick medium thin }
```

Border color receives specification like border-width and refers to sides. It uses the same order and can process one to four values, or each border-color may be specified using border-left (or right, top, or bottom) as it is for width and style. The color setting uses either a color name or an RGB value.

One may also set border style using position (left, right, top, or bottom) and one of the following eight styles: dotted, dashed, solid, double, groove, ridge, inset, outset, or none.

 **Note!**

The final forms for border properties depend upon the user agent. They vary greatly from one browser to another.

The pure `border` property applies the border properties all the way around using the same values. For example, this places a solid red border on all four sides of a paragraph:

```
p { border: solid red }
```

This example does the same but with a lot more text:

```
p {
    border-top: solid red;
    border-right: solid red;
    border-bottom: solid red;
    border-left: solid red
  }
```

However, one can choose to set four different border color, style, and size combinations:

```
p {
    border-top: dotted green thin; border-right:
     solid red thick;
    border-bottom: dashed blue medium;
    border-left: ridge yellow thin
  }
```

Backgrounds

The use of backgrounds in CSS for XML is reminiscent of the HTML property of the same name. Like its HTML counterpart, `background` can be either a color or an image. Additionally, one can set the background image position, whether or not the image repeats, and whether it is fixed relative to the foreground or if it scrolls. The default value for background is `transparent`, so any color applied to the parent will appear to be inherited by the child unless a value is set. The syntax for `background-color` is simple:

```
p { background-color: #F00F00 }
```

The color itself may be an RGB value or a color name (for example, green). In conjunction with background-image properties, a few more properties are available. The most obvious one would be the URI of the desired image. As is always the case, it is necessary to follow the rules for specifying the file location, either via a path on the local server or by means of the fully qualified URI. It is also a good idea to specify a background color as a backup to the image just in case there are issues with the user agent displaying the image.

Remember

With CSS, the background is a style, not a body property as in HTML. Therefore, one can set apart different CSS elements very easily.

The available values for image repetition are repeat (both horizontal and vertical tiling), repeat-x (horizontal), repeat-y (vertical), and no-repeat. The default value is repeat. Here is an example of a background that will have both a color (red) and an image (leafs.gif) that repeats vertically:

```
body {
      background: red URL(leafs.gif);
      background-repeat: repeat-y;
      }
```

To obtain a simple tiling background image, one would use:

```
body { background: red URL (leafs.gif); }
```

and the image would, by default, repeat in both the x and y directions.

The background-attachment property determines whether a background image scrolls with the canvas or remains relatively motionless to the content. The default value is scroll. Adding the background-attachment property to the earlier example, it becomes:

```
body {
        background: red URL(leafs.gif);
        background-repeat: repeat-y;
        background-attachment: fixed
        }
```

In this instance, the background image will remain stationary relative to the content being rendered.

There are several ways to express the `background-position` property. One can use the customary left, right, and center, as well as top, bottom, and center. Another option is to position the image by a percentage of the browser width and height or a length. The horizontal value is specified first, and combinations are allowed. The defaults are 0% 0% (upper left).

The following examples all illustrate legal position declarations:

- `top left` and `left top` are equivalent to `0% 0%`.
- `top`, `top center`, and `center top` are equivalent to `50% 0%`.
- `right`, `top` and `top right` are equivalent to `100% 0%`.
- `left`, `left center`, and `center left` are equivalent to `0% 50%`.
- `center` and `center center` are equivalent to `50% 50%`.
- `right`, `right center`, and `center right` are equivalent to `100% 50%`.
- `bottom left` and `left bottom` are equivalent to `0% 100%`.
- `bottom`, `bottom center`, and `center bottom` are equivalent to `50% 100%`.
- `bottom right` and `right bottom` are equivalent to `100% 100%`

Modify the preceding example by placing the background image in its desired position. The additional text is in boldface:

```
body {
        background: red URL(leafs.gif);
        background-repeat: repeat-y;
        background-attachment: fixed;
        background-position: right top
        }
```

This places the image all the way to the right and at the top of the canvas. One could also declare

```
body {
        background: red URL(leafs.gif);
        background-repeat: repeat-y;
        background-attachment: fixed;
        background-position: 100% 0%
        }
```

and get the same result.

One more way of stating this is:

```
body {
        background: red URL (leafs.gif);
        background-repeat: repeat-y;
        background-attachment: fixed;
        background-position: 100% top
        }
```

Real-World Issues: Using CSS for XML Delivery

To include CSS (either CSS1 or CSS2 and beyond) in an XML document, one simply includes a processing instruction (PI) in the XML document's prologue. For instance to apply the CSS rules in file, a.css, include the following:

```
<?xml-stylesheet type="text/css" href="a.css"?>
```

This PI indicates that the program rendering the XML document should include a CSS file called a.css of the encoding type text/css that is in the same directory as the calling XML document. The usual rules for path/URI information apply.

Remember

The XML processor itself does not deal with the style sheet beyond verifying the syntax of the PI. The software application capable of rendering the XML elements according to the descriptions provided by the CSS rules is responsible.

Whether there is one CSS rule set or many, as long as the processor can locate a file of the same name as the one specified in the PI, the rendering program (usually a browser) will use it. Of course, the rules should be appropriate to the desired display format of the document.

Practically any text editor capable of storing text-only, ASCII files can create a CSS file by storing it with a .css extension. Some of the XML editors listed in Chapter 1 will suffice as excellent CSS editors, as well as any simple ASCII text editor, such as HTML-Kit, EditPlus, or TextPad for the Windows platforms.

The following basic requirements apply when using CSS with XML:

- Embedded style sheets are not allowed.
- Styling as an attribute is not allowed.
- Linking is not allowed (for example, the link element in HTML).
- There must be a PI as illustrated above.

Having adhered to these requirements, one need only open the XML document with a browser or another appropriate rendering program.

Review Questions

Review Question 4.1 What are the three basic types of style that create the cascade in CSS?
Answer: Author, user, user agent (UA).

Review Question 4.2 What is their order of precedence?
Answer: UA overrides user, which overrides author.

Review Question 4.3 What are two components of a declaration?
Answer: Property and value.

Review Question 4.4 Name three subcomponents and provide a brief description of the components that make up XSL.
Answer: XPath, which is a language for referencing specific parts of an XML document; XSLT, which is a language for describing how to transform one XML document (represented as a tree) into another; and XSL, which is XSLT plus a description of a set of formatting objects and formatting properties.

Review Question 4.5 Which of these is *not* one of the eight border styles?
```
dotted
dashed
solid
single
double
groove
ridge
inset
outset
```
Answer: `solid`; all the others are border styles.

Review Question 4.6 What is the default value for background?
  a. `white`
  b. `transparent`
  c. `inherited`
  d. `black`
Answer: b. `transparent`.

Review Question 4.7 Which one of these PI examples is correct?
  a. `<!- xml-stylesheet type="text/css" href= "my_CSS.css" ->`
  b. `<?xml-stylesheet type="text/css" href="my_CSS.css"?>`

c. `<?xml-stylesheet style="text/css"`
   `href="my_CSS.css"?>`
d. `<?xml-stylesheet style="text/css"`
   `href="my_CSS.css"/>`

Answer: b. All the others have syntax errors.

Review Question 4.8 What was added for use with fonts to the CSS specification in CSS2?
Answer: `text-shadow`, `font-size-adjust`, and `font-stretch`.

Review Question 4.9 Give an example of one of the answers from Question 4.8, and explain its use and syntax.
Answer: `h3 { text-shadow: 3px 4px 5px red }`.

Review Question 4.10 What are three properties of the border style?
Answer: b. width, border-style, color.

Solved Problems

Use this example XML document to create a style sheet (CSS) to present it in a Web browser.

```
<cd>
 <title>Beautiful Maladies</title>
 <artist>
 <firstname>Tom</firstname>
 <lastname>Waits</lastname>
 </artist>
 <song genre="urbanfolk" year="1987"
 length="2:42">Hang on St. Christopher</song>
 <song genre="urban folk" year="1987"
 length="3:51">Temptation</song>
 <song genre="urban folk" year="1985"
 length="3:45"> Clap Hands</song>
</cd>
```

Use the following DTD.

```
<!DOCTYPE title [
<!ELEMENT CD (title, artist+, song*)>
<!ELEMENT title (#PCDATA) >
<!ELEMENT artist((firstname*,lastname) |
 group?)>
<!ELEMENT firstname (#PCDATA)>
<!ELEMENT lastname (#PCDATA)>
<!ELEMENT group (#PCDATA)>
<!ELEMENT song (#PCDATA)>
<!ATTLIST song genre CDATA #IMPLIED>
<!ATTLIST song year CDATA #IMPLIED>
<!ATTLIST song length CDATA #IMPLIED>
]>
```

Solved Problem 4.1 Declare a font color of `red` and weight of `400` for the title element.
Solution:
```
title { font-color: red; font-weight: 400}
```
or
```
title { font-color: 255-0-0; font-weight: 400}
```

Solved Problem 4.2 Declare a font size and weight for the song element.
Solution:
```
song { font-size: 14px; font-weight: 400}
```

Solved Problem 4.3 Add the `notes` element and declare the `display: block` style in the DTD.
Solution: Modify the root declaration:
```
<!ELEMENT CD (title, artist+, song*, notes?)>
```
Add this element:
```
<!ELEMENT notes (#PCDATA)>
```
Declare the style rule:
```
notes { display: inline; font-weight: bold }
```

Solved Problem 4.4 Create a text shadow for the artist element.
Solution:
```
artist { text-shadow: 3px 4px 5px red }
```

Solved Problem 4.5 Place all these in a style sheet named cd.css and link it in the XML document by creating the appropriate PI.
Solution: Save in a text editor as cd.css:

```
title { font-color: red; font-weight: 400}
song{ font-size: 14px; font-weight: 400}
notes  {  display:  inline;  font-weight:  bold}
artist { text-shadow: 3px 4px 5px red }
```

Use this PI:

```
<?xml-stylesheet type="text/css" href="cd.css"?>
```

Chapter 5
DOM AND SAX

Levels of DOM

The Document Object Model (DOM) provides a standard set of *objects* and *methods* for representing HTML and XML documents. It creates a standard model for how to combine these objects as well as a standard interface to access and manipulate them. The DOM serves as an application programming interface (API) that allows vendors or authors to write to or support this API instead of creating their own proprietary or product-spe-

cific APIs, therefore increasing the interoperability of the Web. In essence, the DOM defines an important model that programmers can use to help their code interact with XML documents.

The World Wide Web consortium (W3C) governs specifications of the DOM. The DOM represents an XML document as a tree of *nodes* whose order and structure identify the locations of the document's elements. Each node in the tree is randomly and readily accessible. As the middle term of the model's name (object) indicates, the DOM takes documents and arranges their elements to be accessible as objects, following the organization of the document's internal structure. This approach makes the DOM easy to navigate and follow; also, its object orientation makes it familiar to those who use object-oriented languages.

To quote from a W3C Activity Statement:

> W3C's Document Object Model (DOM) is a standard API (application programming interface) to the document structure and aims to make it easy for programmers to access components and delete, add or edit their content, attributes and style. In essence, the DOM makes it possible for programmers to write applications which will work properly on all browsers and servers, and on all platforms. While programmers may need to use different programming languages, they do not need to change their programming model.

The W3C describes the DOM as a "platform- and language-neutral interface that will allow programs and scripts to dynamically access and update the content, structure and style of documents. The document can be further processed, and the resutts of that processing can be incorporated back into the presented page."

The levels of the DOM are still evolving, where each new level builds on preceding levels with increased complexity and versatility. The initial DOM described only a few methods, such as a method to access an identifier by name or through a particular link. Functionality equivalent to that included in Netscape Navigator 3.0 and Microsoft Internet Explorer 3.0 is referred to as DOM level 0.

Level 1, on the other hand, focuses on the core document model, primarily HTML, and provides methods for document navigation and manipulation. The level 1 DOM is the core object model by virtue of its basic functionality. An object model resides in the memory of the user agent, and defines the core tree (node) structure on which subsequent levels build.

Level 2 adds a style sheet object model and defines functionality to manipulate style information attached to a document. It also enables traversal of the document, defines an event model, and provides support for XML namespaces.

Level 3 addresses document loading and saving, as well as content models, such as DTDs and schemas, with document validation support. In addition, level 3 also addresses document views and formatting, key events, and event groups.

Level 4 and beyond should ". . . specify some interface with a possible underlying window system, including some ways to prompt the user. They may also contain a query language interface and address multithreading and synchronization, security, and repository."

At this point, level 3 is at the Working Draft stage, and level 4 and beyond are just speculation. Level 2 became a Recommendation in November of 2000. As a W3C specification, the guiding objective for the XML DOM is to provide a standard programming interface for XML documents for a wide variety of applications. The design goal is for XML DOM to be used with any programming language and any operating system.

Remember

The primary purpose of the DOM is to permit programs to access and manipulate elements in an XML document, based on an attribute value, the absolute or relative location, or the element's name.

XML Tree Structure

With the XML DOM, a programmer can create an XML document, navigate its structure, and add, modify, or delete its elements. The key to understanding and using the DOM is to grasp the underlying tree structure that it builds in the client memory to provide access to the API. The API is the *interface* to the document and allows manipulation of the document during parsing.

The documentElement is the top level of the tree. It may contain many branches, which are referred to as nodes. The *node interface* is the primary datatype for the entire DOM. It represents a single node in the document tree. It may contain a childNode, depending on its definition (not all allow descendants). Examples of nodes that do not allow children are DocumentType, ProcessingInstruction, Comment, Text, and CDATASection. Each of these childNodes represents another tree branch and can be accessed individually via properties and methods. Nodes may be referenced as an *ancestor*, which is any node X above (toward the root) from the node Y. A *descendant* node is any node Z that is below the node Y. A *parent* node is the immediate ancestor node. In addition, two nodes are considered equivalent if they have the same node type and name. Figure 5-1 shows the basic node categories of an XML DOM.

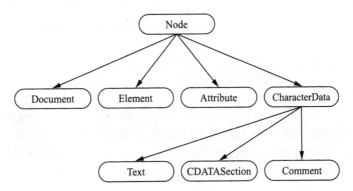

Figure 5-1 The basic node categories of an XML DOM.

A node property will return a value (or list of values) for the node. For instance, the childNodes property returns a NodeList containing all the child nodes for that node. Another property is nodeValue, which returns, or sets, the value of this node, depending on the type. A method allows the node to be manipulated by an operation or function. Table 5-1 shows a list of typical node properties from www .w3schools.com.

Table 5-1 Typical Node Properties

Name	Description
attributes	Returns a NamedNodeMap containing all attributes for this node.
childNodes	Returns a NodeList containing all the child nodes for this node.
firstChild	Returns the first child node for this node.
lastChild	Returns the last child node for this node.
nextSibling	Returns the next sibling node. Two nodes are siblings if they have the same parent node.
nodeName	Returns the nodeName, depending on the type.
nodeType	Returns the nodeType as a number.
nodeValue	Returns, or sets, the value of this node, depending on the type.
ownerDocument	Returns the root node of the document.
parentNode	Returns the parent node for this node.
previousSibling	Returns the previous sibling node. Two nodes are siblings if they have the same parent node.

Table 5-2 presents a generalized list of methods from www.w3schools .com.

In summary:

- Child element A is called the child of element B if and only if element B is the parent of element A.
- Descendant element A is called a descendant of element B if either element A is a child of element B or element A is the child of element C that is a descendant of element B.
- Ancestor element A is called an ancestor of element B if and only if element B is a descendant of element A.
- Sibling element A is called a sibling of element B if and only if

Table 5-2 Methods for Use with Nodes

Name	Descriphon
appendChild(newChild)	Appends the node newChild at the end of the child nodes for this node.
cloneNode(boolean)	Returns an exact clone of this node. If the boolean value is set to true, the cloned node contains all the child nodes as well.
hasChildNodes()	Returns true if this node has any child nodes.
insertBefore(newNode,refNode)	Inserts a new node newNode before the existing node refNode.
removeChild(nodeName)	Removes the node named nodeName.
replaceChild(newNode,oldNode)	Replaces oldNode with the newNode.

elements B and A share the same parent element. Element A is a *preceding sibling* if it comes before element B in the document tree. Element A is a *following sibling* if it comes after element B in the document tree.

The DOM Core

Level 1 of the XML DOM is considered the core of the API. It provides a basic but essential collection of objects and interfaces useful to access and manipulate document objects. Again, the W3C says it best:

The DOM Level 1 specification separates into two parts: Core and HTML. The Core DOM Level 1 section provides a low-level set of fundamental interfaces that can represent any structured document, as well as defining extended interfaces for representing an XML document. These extended XML interfaces need not be implemented by a DOM implementation that only provides access to HTML documents; all of the fundamental interfaces in the Core section must be implemented. A compliant DOM implementation that implements the extended XML interfaces is required to also implement the fundamental Core interfaces, but not the HTML interfaces. The HTML Level I section provides additional, higher-level interfaces that are used with the fundamental interfaces defined in the Core Level I section to provide a more convenient view of an HTML document. A compliant implementation of the HTML DOM implements all of the fundamental Core interfaces as well as the HTML interfaces.

Remember that the Document Object Model represents an XML document as a tree or hierarchy of node objects, where other more specialized interfaces are also available. The node interface is the primary datatype for the entire DOM. It represents a single node in the document tree. Although all objects implementing the node interface expose methods for dealing with children, not all objects implementing the node interface may have children. Some types of nodes may have child nodes of various types, and others may be leaf nodes that cannot have anything below them in the document structure. The node types and the node types that they may have as children are as follows:

- *Document.* Element (there is a maximum of one), ProcessingInstruction, Comment, and DocumentType.
- *DocumentFragment.* Element, Comment, Text, ProcessingInstruction, EntityReference, and CDATASection.
- *EntityReference.* Element, ProcessingInstruction, Comment, CDATASection, EntityReference, and Text.
- *Element.* Element, Text, Comment, EntityReference, CDATASection, and ProcessingInstruction.
- *Attr.* Text and EntityReference.

- *Entity.* `Element`, `ProcessingInstruction`, `Comment`, `Text`, `CDATASection`, and `EntityReference`.

`DocumentType`, `CDATASection`, `Notation`, `Comment`, `Text`, and `ProcessingInstruction`, may not have any children.

Using DOM Interfaces

Beyond manual editing and translation of XML documents, it will be useful for the user to manipulate XML content using DOM calls. This is the point the DOM interface comes into play. By accessing properties of the DOM through its various methods, one can create a platform-independent and language-neutral interface. This interface is a precursor to more complex APIs such as SAX. Most of these properties and methods are present in DOM level 0 or 1 and, as a result, are widely available for most applications.

The term *object* in the Document Object Model may be a bit misleading, much like the *Java* in JavaScript. The properties of the DOM are not accessed as objects in the truest sense, but rather through the interface.

Consider the following simple example as a way of investigating the DOM interface:

```
<parent>
 <child name="child1">
  text to display
 </child>
</parent>
```

Figure 5-2 shows how the DOM represents the previous markup.

The DOM interface and its properties and methods provide the means of accessing the individual node. For example, to extract the contents of the element

```
<child name="child1">text to display</child>
```

one can use the `getNodeValue()` method, accomplishing this by a series of steps that access the properties and values along the way. The ac-

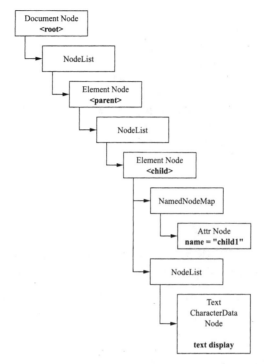

Figure 5-2 Markup `<parent><child name="child1">text to display</child></parent>` as represented in the DOM.

tual code depends on the XML parser in use, such as Sun TreeWalker or MSXML.

The first step is to bring in the document via the DOM interface using `Node`. The node is the heart of the DOM interface and is a logical and likely starting point. The methods used to accomplish this are `get-NodeName()`, which returns the name of the node, `getNodeValue()`, which returns the value of the node, `hasChildNodes()`, which returns a Boolean true or false, `getFirstChild()`, and `get-NextSibling()`.

If there are children, that is, if `hasChildNodes()=true`, one can use them as stepping-stones or waypoints to navigate the node structure of the document. From here, it is possible to call `get-`

FirstChild() and getNextSibling(). Using only these two methods, it is easy to traverse the entire tree. Other additional methods like getLastChild(), getPreviousSibling(), and getParentNode() provide convenience when returning to the top of the tree and are very handy on a document of any size.

Thus, one can start at the <parent> node, test for children, and use getFirstChild(). It is then possible to call method getNodeName(), and if it is the desired node, to then call getNodeValue(). If the name of the node is not the desired one, the next logical step is to call getNextSibling().

Note!

A DOM interface is a language-independent description of a DOM structure. By referencing the interface, a program can define and manipulate DOM structures.

DOM Traversal and Ranges

The navigation, or stepping from node to node within the XML document by the parser, is known as *traversing*. The DOM provides tools in the API for ordered movement between nodes and their ancestors, children, and siblings. A *range* indicates the content contained between two specified end points as one contiguous selection. A range interface confers the advantage of being able to access and manipulate entire portions of a document tree at a higher-level, rather than requiring the decomposition of the range into a sequence of separately handled nodes. See the W3C DOM core for full details.

A range consists of two *boundary points* representing the start and end of the range. The positions of the boundary points in a document (or DocumentFragment) tree consist of a starting node address and an offset (or range of nodes within the DOM's internal tree structure). The starting node address becomes the container for the boundary point and its position in the tree. This container and its ancestors are also ancestors to the boundary point and its position in the tree as well, so they are available for navigation purposes. Likewise, the offset of a node becomes the offset of the boundary point and its position in the tree. If the container node is of type `Attr`, `Document`, `DocumentFragment`, `Element`, or `EntityReference`, that offset occurs before its child nodes, but if the container node is of type `CharacterData`, `Comment`, or `ProcessingInstruction` (PI), the offset occurs before the string value for the node.

The boundary points of a range must share a common ancestor, which is either a `Document`, `DocumentFragment`, or `Attr` node. That is, the content of a range must be entirely within the subtree rooted by a single `Document`, `DocumentFragment`, or `Attr` node. This common ancestor container is known as the *root container* of the range. The tree rooted by the root container is known as the range's *context tree*.

When navigating XML documents, the traversal-range recommendation defines two separate interfaces for XML elements. The `NodeIterator` interface provides methods to move linearly through a document, traversing it from node to node in the order in which they occur. The `TreeWalker` interface permits traversal of the document as a tree-based structure. To use either of these interfaces, call the `create` method and set appropriate flags for elements that should be included in the view.

In practice, one would use an application such as Xerces (available from the Apache Software Foundation), which is a Java application that has all the needed files and plenty of documentation. Others are available, of course, from Microsoft, Sun, and other vendors.

To traverse a flat representation of XML, use the `NodeIterator` interface. For example, look at the following XML document which is derived from an example that resides at the site: http://www.onjava.com/pub/a/onjava/2001/02/08/dom.html?page=2:

```
<a>
 <b>first text</b>
 <c>
  <d>a child of c</d>
  <e>another child of c, sibling to d</e>
 </c>
 <f>some more text</f>
```

```
<g>still more text</g>
</a>
```

When flattened, it gives the nodes: a b c d e f g. Traversal of these nodes, yields what is called a *horizontal version* of the XML document.

The other approach is to use the `TreeWalker` interface, which allows one to approach the tree structure of the XML document using the parent and child nodes. The `TreeWalker` interface provides the methods for jumping from node to node via `parentNode()`, `firstChild()`, `lastChild()`, `previousSibling()`, `nextSibling()`, and so on, as well as the more linear `previousNode()` and `nextNode()`. As discussed in the section on using DOM interfaces, it is possible to traverse the entire XML document using just `firstChild()` and `nextSibling()`. However, it is most practical to take advantage of the convenience offered by the full list of methods.

The `TreeWalker` interface, parses the entire XML document by traversing each branch of the tree in turn using `nextNode()` as the primary method. The output from this method is often identical to the `NodeIterator` interface with the hierarchy of the original tree retained. Since some nodes may be missing, it also has methods to move up and down in the tree as well as back and forth.

The SAX Interface

SAX, the *Simple API for XML*, is a standard interface for event-based XML parsing, whereas the DOM interface is tree-based. SAX produces a tree of `xmlNode` structures that the parser traverses.

SAX is most effective for processing a small subset of a large XML document. SAX allows one to efficiently locate specific parts of the document without the processing time required for creating a tree view, as required in the DOM interface.

SAX is event-based, so when the SAX parser comes to a specified element in the XML document, it treats it like an event and calls the appropriate code for that event. The SAX parser uses callback methods that run when a specific item has been found in the document. Some of the more common callbacks are `startDocument`, `endDocument`, `startElement`, `endElement`, `getEntity`, and `characters`. Most of these are fairly self-explanatory. The `characters` callback executes when characters outside a tag are parsed.

As of this writing, SAX 2.0.1 is the current implementation. In addition, SAX is not a full XML parser but rather a set of Java interfaces and helper classes that any parser that wants to be compliant with SAX 2.0.1 must implement. SAX is most appropriate for XML and Java, although it can also work with Python, Perl, or C++.

The SAX 2.0.1 interfaces, classes, and exceptions are:

Package org.xml.sax
Interfaces
- `Attributes`
- `ContentHandler`
- `DTDHandler`
- `EntityResolver`
- `ErrorHandler`
- `Locator`
- `XMLFilter`
- `XMLReader`

Classes
- `InputSource`

Exceptions
- `SAXException`
- `SAXNotRecognizedException`
- `SAXNotSupportedException`
- `SAXParseException`

Package org.xml.sax.helpers
Classes
- `AttributesImpl`
- `DefaultHandler`
- `LocatorImpl`
- `NamespaceSupport`
- `ParserAdapter`
- `XMLFilterImpl`
- `XMLReaderAdapter`
- `XMLReaderFactory`

The most important and immediately useful of these are the different handler interfaces (that is, `ContentHandler`, `DTDHandler`, etc.).

The `ContentHandler` interface, for example, specifies all the callback methods that will deliver information about:

- The *document* starting and ending elements
- An XML element's starting and ending points
- Namespaces and attributes for elements
- Namespace prefix mapping
- Processing instructions
- White space and character data

There are four main handlers in SAX:

- `EntityResolver`
- `DTDHandler`
- `DocumentHandler`
- `ErrorHandler`

`DocumentHandler` contains the following methods:

- `public abstract void startDocument()` throws a `SAXException` error.
- `public abstract void endDocument()` throws a `SAXException` error.
- `public abstract void startElement(String name, AttributeList atts)` throws a `SAXException` error.
- `public abstract void endElement(String name)` throws a `SAXException` error.

These declare scope (public), datatype, and the like. When working with handlers, it is necessary to implement the abstract functions of the handler, instantiate a new handler, and set the handler to the parser.

To use SAX to read XML, one must create a parser object instance that points to the XML document and to the application. While SAX reads the document, it calls the `startElement` (the start tag), `endElement` (the end tag), and `characters` (text data in between) as it goes.

The SAX parser reads the XML file (also a DTD if it is present), and when it encounters something such as an element, it generates an event. The program can register with the parser as a listener to such an event by implementing certain interfaces. The SAX parser then calls standard methods, which the program has overridden, to respond to the event. Although the SAX parser organizes its events a bit differently, the situation is similar to an Abstract Window Toolkit (AWT) button generating `ActionEvents` when clicked. Then an interested class implements an `ActionListener` and overrides the callback method `actionPerformed`.

SAX events, unlike AWT events, come in an ordered sequence as the XML file reads in. Given the tree structure of the XML file, the parser generates events in a *depth-first* order. Furthermore, because the events trigger on the fly as the XML file reads in, there is only one chance to grab an event as it goes by. The program must do something to capture relevant information at the point at which it arrives or the information is lost for the current pass of the parser through the file. This is in contrast to the DOM parser, which reads the entire document in, storing it in its tree structure in memory, and then waits for the program to analyze it.

The steps are:

1. Obtain a SAX parser (such as Xerces from Apache).
2. Provide a document handler (usually a Java class).
3. Customize error handling for the software used (also Java-based).
4. Use a validating parser for the XML (Xerces again).

To understand how an event-based API works, consider the following sample document:

```
<?xml version="1.0"?>
<doc>
<greeting>Hi everyone!</greeting>
</doc>
```

An event-based interface will break the structure of this document into a series of linear events:

```
start document
start element: doc
start element: greeting
characters: Hello everyone!
```

```
end element: greeting
end element: doc
end document
```

Here is an example of a simple Java SAX routine to generate the preceding output from the sample document:

```
import org.xml.sax.HandlerBase;
import org.xml.sax.AttributeList;
public class MyHandler extends HandlerBase
{
   public void startElement(String name,
                              AttributeList atts)
   {
    System.out.println("Start element: " + name);
   }
   public void endElement (String name)
   {
     System.out.println("End element: " + name);
   }
}
```

Review Questions

Review Question 5.1 What does the DOM use for accessing and manipulating objects in the document?
> a. Properties and methods
> b. Attributes and elements
> c. Comments
> d. Processing instructions

Answer: Properties and methods.

Review Question 5.2 Is the DOM specific to any particular platform or operating system?
Answer: No, it is a "platform-neutral and language-neutral interface."

Review Question 5.3 Which level of the DOM is considered the core?
Answer: Level 1 is the core, and levels 2 and beyond build on that level.

Review Question 5.4 The DOM is considered to be what type of structure?
  a. Branching
  b. Linear
  c. Tree
  d. Text
Answer: c. The DOM is a tree structure.

Review Question 5.5 Which of the following cannot contain children?
  a. `DocumentType`
  b. `ProcessingInstruction`
  c. `Comment`
  d. `Text`
  e. `CDATA Section`
  f. `Notation`
  g. All of the above
  h. None of the above
Answer: g. All of the above cannot have child nodes.

Review Question 5.6 What is the node B directly above node A called?
  a. Father
  b. Mother
  c. Ancestor
  d. Child
Answer: c. Ancestor

Review Question 5.7 What are nodes that share a common ancestor called?
  a. Cousins
  b. Siblings
  c. Related
  d. Friends
Answer: b. Sibling nodes

Review Question 5.8 What is the content contained between two end points called?
  a. Range
  b. Content
  c. Traverse
  d. All of the above
Answer: a. Range is the content contained between two end points.

Review Question 5.9 What are the two types of traversal methods?
Answer: `TreeWalker` and `NodeIterator`

Review Question 5.10 When using a `TreeWalker` interface,
    a. the program parses the entire XML document by traversing each branch of the tree.
    b. the program parses only some of the XML document's nodes.
    c. the program parse siblings.
    d. the program walks the parents
Answer: a. the entire XML document is parsed by traversing each branch of the tree.

Review Question 5.11 Is the output from the `TreeWalker` different from that of the `NodeIterator`?
Answer: No, the output from the `TreeWalker` interface is often identical to the `NodeIterator` interface with the hierarchy of the original tree retained.

Review Question 5.12 Is one method (`TreeWalker` versus `NodeIterator`) better than the other?
Answer: No, they both have their strong points. The `TreeWalker` allows more freedom to move forward and back, and the `NodeIterator` is better suited to large documents.

Review Question 5.13 On what is the SAX interface based?
    a. Events
    b. Trees
    c. Elements
    d. Nodes
Answer: SAX is a standard interface for event-based XML parsing.

Review Question 5.14 What makes up the SAX package?
    a. Interfaces
    b. Classes
    c. Exceptions
    d. All of the above
Answer: d. All of the above

Review Question 5.15 What are the four main handlers in the SAX interface?

Answer: EntityResolver, DTDHandler, DocumentHand-
ler, and ErrorHandler

Solved Problem

In the problem below, use the DTD and XML document of Chapter 2:

```
<!ELEMENT motionpicture(title, year, genre,
  director)>

<!ELEMENT title (#PCDATA)>
<!ATTLIST title language CDATA #IMPLIED>
<!ATTLIST title alternate_title CDATA #IMPLIED>
<!ATTLIST title country CDATA #IMPLIED>
<!ATTLIST title certification #IMPLIED>
<!ATTLIST title runtime #IMPLIED>

<!ELEMENT year (#PCDATA)>
<!ATTLIST year academy_awards CDATA #IMPLIED>
<!ATTLIST year distributor CDATA #IMPLIED>

<!ELEMENT genre (#PCDATA)>
<!ATTLIST genre category CDATA #IMPLIED>
<!ATTLIST genre medium CDATA #IMPLIED>

<!ELEMENT director (#PCDATA)>
<!ATTLIST director director_of_photography
  CDATA> #IMPLIED>
<!ATTLIST director cinematographer
  CDATA #IMPLIED>
<!ATTLIST director editor CDATA #IMPLIED>
```

Solved Problem 5.1 What would the output be as a flat representation?
Solution: The output as a horizontal representation of the elements would
be

```
motionpicture title year genre director
```

The elements, but not the attributes, undergo parsing. The entire representation consists of elements, starting at the top, or root, and migrating
from there.

Chapter 6
XPATH

Location Paths

The XML Path Language (XPath) is a declarative language defined by the World Wide Web Consortium (W3C) and used to traverse the Document Object Model based on the DOM's tree-node structure. XPath is a mechanism to identify and access portions or subsets of XML documents. XPath uses a path-based syntax that is very similar to the traversal syntax used in file systems or document retrieval. XPath is a direct result of the needs of addressing used in the Extensible Stylesheet Language Transformations (XSLT, covered in Chapter 7). It provides a common foundation for solving a  fundamental problem, which is the need to locate elements, attributes, and other XML document nodes in a concise and convenient way.

According to the W3C, XPath's primary purpose is to address parts of an XML document. It also provides basic facilities for manipulation of strings, numbers, and Booleans. XPath uses a compact, non-XML syntax to facilitate use of XPath within URIs and XML attribute values. XPath operates on the abstract, logical structure of an XML document rather than on its surface syntax.

The key concept to XPath is the *location path*. This allows almost a trickle-down or cascading technique, where each node of the location path is indicated in a directory-like fashion, familiar to anyone with a DOS or UNIX background. The node tree replaces the tree of the directory, but the syntax similarity between them is very consistent. Each node of the tree has one of the following *node types*:

- Document
- Element
- Attribute
- Text
- Namespace
- Processing instruction
- Comment

The basic construct of the location path is a sequence of location steps separated by a slash (/). A location path evaluates compositionally left-to-right, starting with some initial context.

Each node resulting from the evaluation of one step serves as context for evaluation of the next step, and the results string together. For the examples of location path syntax, start with a document with the node (element) structure that appears in Figure 6-1.

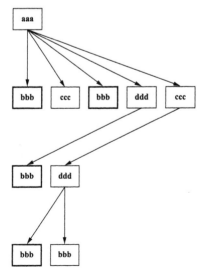

Figure 6-1 Node element structure.

Remember

The primary purpose of the XPath is to identify sets of nodes in the XML document that satisfy particular selection criteria.

In XML, this looks like:

```
<aaa>
 <bbb/>
 <ccc/>
 <bbb/>
 <ddd>
  <bbb/>
 </ddd>
 <ccc>
  <ddd>
   <bbb/>
   <bbb/>
  </ddd>
 </ccc>
</aaa>
```

If the path starts with a slash (/), it represents an absolute path to the required element. An easy example is /aaa, which selects the root element aaa and looks similar to Figure 6-2.

Another simple example is /aaa/ddd/bbb, which selects all elements bbb that are children of ddd that are children of the root element aaa, as shown in Figure 6-3.

Or another example is //bbb, which selects all bbb elements, as shown in Figure 6-4.

Another example is /aaa/ccc, which selects all elements ccc that are children of the root element aaa, as shown in Figure 6-5.

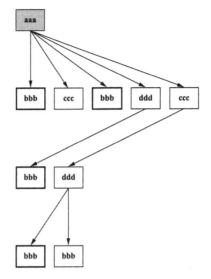

Figure 6-2 The root element selected.

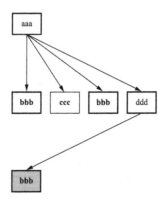

Figure 6-3 All bbb elements that are children of ddd selected.

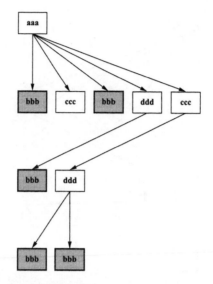

Figure 6-4 All bbb elements selected.

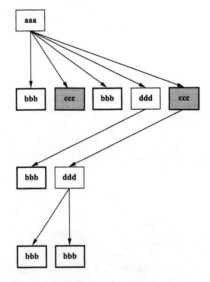

Figure 6-5 All ccc elements selected.

Location Path Axes and Node Tests

Location path syntax frequently refers to axes, which correspond to relationships between nodes that allow navigation as a reference to the current node, no matter which one it might be. An axis identifies a set of nodes that have some relationship to the context node.

The axes available in XPath are shown in Table 6-1 (based on the current, or *context,* node).

Table 6-1 Available XPath Axes

Axis	Nodes Matched
child	Children of the context node
descendant	All descendants
parent	Parent (or direct ancestor)
ancestor	All ancestors between the root and the current parent node
sibling	Nodes with a shared parent
following-sibling	Siblings to the *right* of the context node
preceding-sibling	Siblings to the *left* of the context node
following	The nodes whose opening tags follow the context node's closing tag in the XML document but which are not descendents of it, attribute nodes, or namespace nodes.
preceding	The nodes whose closing tags precede the context node's opening tag in the XML document but which are not ancestors of it, attribute nodes, or namespace nodes
self	The context node itself
descendent-or-self	The context node and its descendent
ancestor-or-self	The context node and its ancestor

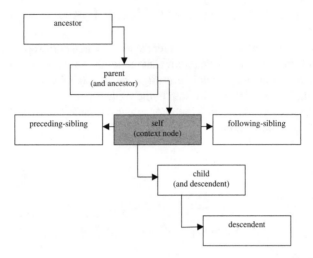

Figure 6-6 A schematic of path axis relationships.

Figure 6-6 shows a schematic of these path axis relationships. One can specify any navigational need using this syntax. The figure demonstrates that it is possible to reach each node from any other node using location path syntax.

XPath supports *node-tests* to select specific nodes along a particular axis. Table 6-2 lists some of these tests and their descriptions.

One separates the axis form the test using the double colon (: :) symbol. Table 6-3 illustrates some location steps that use node-tests on the

Table 6-2 Node-tests

Test	Nodes Selected
`*`	All nodes on the axis that have the same node type as the axis.
`node()`	All nodes on the axis
`comment()`	All comment nodes on the axis.
`processing-instruction()`	All processing instruction nodes on the axis.
`text()`	All text nodes on the axes.
`node name`	Selects the node that has the name.

Table 6-3 Node-tests in Location Paths

Test	Node Set
`/aaa/child::text()`	Selects all `text` nodes that are children of `aaa`. Empty.
`/aaa/ddd/following::*`	Selects the nodes that follow ddd: `ccc`, `ddd`, `bbb`, `bbb`.
`/aaa/child::comment()`	Selects `comment` nodes of `aaa`. Empty.
`/aaa/bbb/attribute::time`	Selects the `time` attributes of all `bbb` children of `aaa`. Empty
`/aaa/child::*/child::*`	Selects `bbb` and `ddd`, the grandchildren of `aaa`.

data in the example for this chapter. In some cases, the resulting node sets are empty.

Table 6-4 lists some abbreviations used in XPath syntax. These abbreviations serve to shorten the expression of location paths.

Table 6-4 Location Path Abbreviations

Abbreviation	Symbols Replaced
`/` (no axis designator)	`/child::`
`.`	`self::node()`
`@`	`attribute::`
`//`	`/descendant-or-self::node()/`
`..`	`parent::node`

Predicates

In its most general form, an XPath location consists of a set of location steps with step pairs, separated by `/`. Each location step takes the form:

```
axis::node-test[predicate]
```

Previous paragraphs have dealt with axes and node-tests. A predicate is a Boolean value that further restricts the set of nodes that the location step specifies. It does so by removing otherwise qualifying nodes that have a false value for the predicate. XPath locations often make use of the pipe symbol (|) to describe the *logical or* of multiple predicates. They also make frequent use the following *node-set functions*:

- id(string) The element whose id attribute has the value string.
- position() The node's location number within in the node-set.
- last() The number of nodes in the node-set.

Table 6-5 illustrates some path locations that use predicates to establish node sets for the example data used previously in this chapter.

Table 6-5 Predicate Examples

Test	Node Set
/aaa/child::*[position()=1]	Selects the first child of aaa.
/aaa/child::*[position()=2]	Selects the second child of aaa.
/aaa/child::*[position()%lt;3]	Selects the children of aaa in positions 1 and 2.
/aaa/[attribute::time != "0035"]	Select all children of aaa whose time attribute does not have the value "0035".
/aaa/[@time != "0035"]	Selects all children of aaa whose time attribute does not have the value "0035".
/aaa/ccc/ddd[.="f"]/..	Selects all ccc children of aaa that have a ddd child with value "f".
/aaa/[last()]	Selects the last child of aaa.

The following example of the function `id()` demonstrates how a node set function can access an element either by name or by a combination of name and path. The function `id()` has the definition:

```
node-set id (object).
```

One can obtain a `title` element with the function call:

```
id("title")
```

This will return, or select, the element with the unique ID of `title`. Alternatively, the following selects an object offset from the specified `title` element:

```
id("title")/child::subtitle[position=4]
```

which will return the fourth child `subtitle` of the element `title` as a specific element and relative position.

Remember!

The general form for an XPath location consists of one or more location steps of the form:
`axis::node-test[predicate]`
where `axis::` is optional and a slash (/) separates all consecutive location steps.

Review Questions

Review Question 6.1 The context referred to in a location path consists of
   a. context node.
   b. context position and size.
   c. variable bindings.
   d. all of the above.
   e. none of the above.
Answer: d. all of the above. The context consists of a context node, a context position and size, variable bindings, and an initial context.

Review Question 6.2 Which of the following symbols are used in XPath?

    a. / /
    b. ?
    c. \
    d. /
    e. .

Answer: a, d, and e. The ? and \ are not part of the XPath syntax.

Review Question 6.3 Which of the following characters indicates root?

    a. / /
    b. ?
    c. \
    d. /
    e. .

Answer: d. The / is the symbol for root.

Review Question 6.4 What is the meaning of the term axes?

    a. The relationship between the start and end of a document
    b. The relationship between nodes of a document
    c. The relationship between two documents

Answer: b. Axes refer to the relationship between the nodes of a document.

Review Question 6.5 Name five axes used in XPath.
Answer: The axes are child, descendant, parent, ancestor, sibling, following sibling, preceding sibling, following, preceding, self, descendent or self, and ancestor or self.

Solved Problems

Using Figure 6-7, identify the following using the node letter codes.

Solved Problem 6.1 Child of ccc.
Solution: ddd

Solved Problem 6.2 Descendants of ccc.
Solution: ddd, bbb

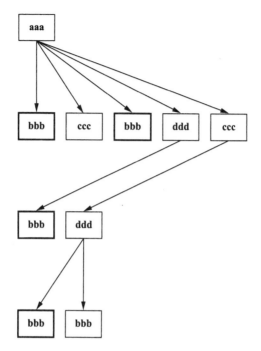

Figure 6-7

Solved Problem 6.3 Parent of ccc.
Solution: aaa

Solved Problem 6.4 Ancestors of ccc.
Solution: aaa

Solved Problem 6.5 Siblings of ccc.
Solution: bbb, ddd

Solved Problem 6.6 Following sibling of ccc.
Solution: bbb, ddd

Solved Problem 6.7 Preceding sibling of ccc.
Solution: bbb, ddd

116 XML

Solved Problem 6.8 Following of ccc.
Solution: ddd, bbb

Solved Problem 6.9 Preceding of ccc.
Solution: bbb

Solved Problem 6.10 Self of ccc.
Solution: ccc

Solved Problem 6.11 Descendant or self of ccc.
Solution: ccc, ddd, bbb

Solved Problem 6.12 Ancestor or self of ccc.
Solution: ccc, aaa

Chapter 7
XSL and XSLT

Use of XPath in XSL

Earlier chapters presented XML as a content-driven markup language. Now it is time to apply the presentation to the content.

The Extensible Stylesheet Language (XSL) applies XML styling (that is, presentation) to XML. The Extensible Stylesheet Language Transformations (XSLT) combine the XML with CSS to create a document that renders through a Web browser or other user agent (UA).

The process of styling requires an XML source document that contains the information to be displayed and a style sheet to define and describe the document's presentation. In the XML document, there are processing instructions (PIs) that declare the XSL document to be used in CSS and its location or URI.

XSLT uses XPath as a means to create a result tree from the source tree (the XML document) and the instruction tree of the XSLT document. Chapter 6 discussed how to specify a node. XPath enables the traversal of the XML document tree and provides access to the subsections of the document. XSLT uses XPath to specify where information is stored in the source (XML) file. XSL also uses it to establish notation from the XSLT file for styling information. XSLT inspects the XPath nodes for style attributes using parent, ancestor, sibling, and the other available axes. XPath allows XSLT to decide whether a given element or attribute appears in a given node or context.

The XSLT Transformation Process

The XSLT process consists of two main steps. The first is called tree transformation, and it takes the XML and XSL documents as input and generates a result tree based on the instructions contained in the XSL file. This might include filtering information (specifying nodes to include or not include) or reordering XML data into a more presentable layout before applying the final style attributes at the time of rendering.

The steps involved include:

1. An XML parser interprets the XML document and forms a tree.
2. The tree passes as input to an XSLT processor.
3. The XSLT processor compares the nodes in the tree with the instructions contained in the referenced style sheet (XSL).
4. When the XSLT processor finds a match, it outputs a tree fragment (result tree).
5. A UA receives the tree in a format such as HTML, speech, or text.

While CSS uses rules to establish what is styled and how it is styled, XSL associates templates with XML elements. An XSL template uses a match attribute to indicate the template needed (of which there can be several) and then creates a transformation from there.

Remember

The major function of XSL is to define what data to present from the XML file and to organize it in a form that a user agent can recognize and process.

The simple motion picture example from Chapter 2 lends itself to using an XSL style sheet and applying it for HTML output. Here is the XML:

```
<?xml version="1.0"?>
<?xml-stylesheet type="text:xsl"
 href="filmlibrary.xsl"?>
<filmlibrary>
 <motionpicture>
  <title>"The Wizard of Oz"</title>
  <year>1939</year>
  <genre category="musical"></genre>
 </motionpicture>
 <motionpicture>
  <title>"Duck Soup"</title>
  <year>1933</year>
  <genre category="comedy"></genre>
 </motionpicture>
 <motionpicture>
  <title>"Gone With the Wind"</title>
  <year>1939</year>
  <genre category="drama"></genre>
 </motionpicture>
</filmlibrary>
```

Next, create a transformation template as an XSL style sheet in a file called filmlibrary.xsl:

```
<?xml version="1.0"?>
 <xsl:stylesheet
  xmlns:xsl="http://www.w3.org/TR/WD-xsl">
 <xsl:template match="/">
  <html>
  <head>
   <title>Film Library</title>
  </head>
   <body>
    <table border="2" bgcolor="white">
     <tr>
      <th>Title</th>
      <th>Genre</th>
      <th>Year</th>
     <tr>
     <xsl:for-each
      select="filmlibrary/motionpicture">
     <tr>
      <td><xsl:value-of select=
      "title"/></td>
      <td><xsl:value-of select=
      "genre"/></td>
      <td><xsl:value-of select="year"/></td>
     </tr>
     </xsl:for-each>
    </table>
   </body>
  </html>
 </xsl:template>
</xsl:stylesheet>
```

Except for the references to <xsl:for-each select~ "film-library/motionpicture">, the code looks remarkably like plain old HTML. In fact, since the target user application is a browser, the file really consists of a CSS style document with an embedded XSL style template. When encountering a title, genre, or year within a filmlibrary/motionpicture element, the template captures the value and writes it as HTML.

The heart of the template is in the element:

```
<xsl:for-each
select="filmlibrary/motionpicture">
.

.

.
</xsl:for-each>
```

This loops through the XML source tree, finds all of the objects possessing the sought-for names, and creates one row for each motionpicture match. The loop runs until no more matches occur. Therefore, the table created here will have only three rows. However, if the source file were a list of the 100 films, it then would generate 100 table rows.

The last step in this short example is to link the two files. The original XML document accomplished this with the PI:

```
<?xml-stylesheet type="text/xsl"
 href="filmlibrary.xsl"?>
```

This statement assumes that the XSL file is called filmlibrary.xsl. Standard syntax for the URI path applies to XSL as well. The final XML output then looks like Figure 7-1 (using Cooktop 2000, an excellent freeware editor).

To better understand the flexibility of the for-each statement, one can change the order of the searched elements in the XSL. In the spirit of separating content from presentation, this changes the entire formatting of the output.

It is possible to reverse the presentation of year and genre by simply changing the XSL template to:

```
<xsl:for-each
 select="filmlibrary/motionpicture">
<tr>
 <td><xsl:value-of select=
  "title"/></td>
 <td><xsl:value-of select="year"/></td>
```

122 XML

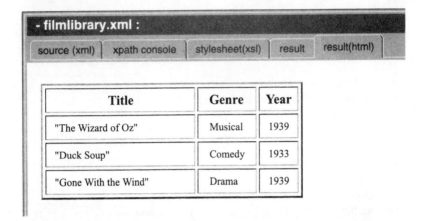

Figure 7-1 XML output after applying an XSL style sheet for the motion picture example from Chapter 2.

```
<td><xsl:value-of select=
 "genre"/></td>
 </tr>
</xsl:for-each>
```

Figure 7-2 shows the second result.

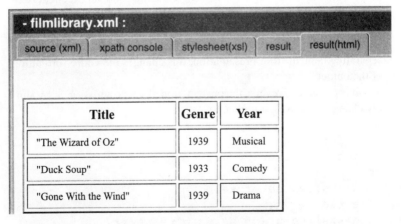

Figure 7-2 Reversing year and genre for the motion picture example.

XSLT Variables, Expressions, and Datatypes

Datatypes in XSL and XSLT are consistent with those found in the other languages of the XML family. The types are not strongly cast but, as in JavaScript or other dynamically typed languages, are forgiving. The types listed in the XSL 1.0 W3C Recommendation are string, number, Boolean, node-set, and tree. Each of these datatypes has been discussed before, but a short review might be in order.

- *String*. Characters (letters, numbers, etc.) that are not used in numeric or arithmetic calculations. If desired, one can use the function `eval()` to convert strings to numbers. Any sequence of characters is allowed as a string in XML.
- *Number*. An integer or floating-point numeric value,
- *Boolean*. A `true` or `false` value.
- *Node-set*. A set of nodes from the source tree.
- *Tree*. The root node and children of the result tree, as defined in XSLT.

Variables are available in two flavors: *global* and *local*. Global variables are available throughout an entire XSLT style sheet, but the local variables are limited to the template that creates them. The manner in which a variable is declared determines the variable's scope.

Variable definition uses the `<xsl:variable>` element to set both the name of the variable and a select value; for example:

```
<xsl:variable name="text_color" select="red">
```

Every subsequent use of the `$text-color` name provides the (string) value red.

Returning to the scoping part of the variable definition process:

- If the `xsl:variable` element resides at the top level of the style sheet as a child (not just a descendant) of the `xsl:stylesheet` element, then its variable has global scope.
- If its declaration occurs within the `xsl:template` element, its variable has local scope.

Thus, it is best to declare and initialize variables that require global access at the beginning of the document using the `xsl:variable` element immediately after the `xsl:stylesheet` element, even if the variable access might not take place until much later in the document. Because datatyping is not critical, it is only necessary to provide a reference to the variable name and an initial value (specified with `select`).

Important!

When defining variables, be careful to avoid reserved words and to follow standard naming practices.

Expressions in XSLT follow the syntax used in XPath. The use of an expression allows one to evaluate a variable or the context of a node. Expressions consist of a *variable reference,* which evaluates to the value bound to a variable name, or a *function call,* which calls a named function and allows the passing of arguments or testing of the context node as a default and returns a value.

In the case of a function call, the returned value datatype depends upon the function, and an error may result if the chosen function is not appropriate. For example, a string value results from a string function, and a `true` or `false` results from a Boolean function type. If one attempts to interchange them, trouble (in the form of errors) is the guaranteed result. The Boolean is valuable when used with a conditional expression, such as equal to, greater or less than, or logical (such as `or`, `and`, or `not` or a combination of these.

Another type of expression used in XSLT (and XPath) is the *pattern.* Patterns are a limited form of location path used to describe a step-by-step path needed to reach a desired node from the context node of a given element. The pattern comparison is an implied Boolean, returning `true` (a match) if the match is found and `false` (or empty) if it is not.

Using the combination of the attribute `match` (or `select`) and a value for a pattern allows comparison of a node for contextual validity and relative location in reference to the current node. Examples based on an `aaa/ccc` location path statement could be `match="/aaa/ccc"` or `select="/aaa/ccc"`. They both specify all elements `ccc` that are children of the root element `aaa`.

Patterns are acceptable alone or in combinations of multiple statements using the proper characters and syntax, such as the | to delineate alternates, and so on. Patterns frequently provide values in a `select` attribute in XSL or as a `match` for node sets, This flexibility permits one to search elements as paths or as pattern matches.

In practice, expressions consist of variables, conditionals, and functions. Table 7-1 shows the characters used in expressions to define node context and node sets.

Table 7-1 Characters Used in Path Expressions

Character	Description
/	Root node
/ /	Descendant (or self node
.	Self node
. .	Parent node

Additionally, XSLT uses all XPath axes.

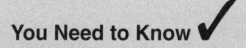

You Need to Know ✔

In XSL expressions:
- a. Datatypes are dynamic, not strongly cast.
- b. Variables are declarative (cannot be updated).
- c. Variables are local or global depending on when (and where) they are defined.
- d. Expressions use XPath syntax.
- e. Core functions are used in the same manner as in XPath, with the same syntax and datatype restraints.

A style sheet usually provides the markup needed to present a document, whether it is intended for a Web browser, personal digital assistant

(PDA), or text-to-speech device. The structure of the style sheet depends upon the three main elements of a presentable document:

- Content
- Layout
- Style

The content, of course, resides in the XML document, which will generate the source tree and undergo validation by the XML parser, but the quality of the content itself is left up to the document author. As is always the case in XML, the content exists independently of any presentation markup. Extra attention paid to maintaining clean, clear XML content will pay off when the time comes to transform the document. It is important to keep the content/presentation relationship as pure as possible, even though the temptation may be there to do otherwise.

The layout determines the way in which the information is presented to the viewer or user agent, how the content is organized, and how the document flows. This step is critical and requires a good amount of thought for anything beyond a simple, dry text document. At this point, content and presentation begin to merge to form the output document. The transition is not yet complete, but elements of both are now present at the XSL processor, and the trees are forming. Remember that the transformation style sheet contains only presentation instructions and that the content may change based on the XML file being transformed; in other words, the style sheet is still somewhat of a moving target.

Remember

The transformation style sheet contains only presentation instructions and the content may change based on the XML file being transformed. The stylesheet must be general enough to deal with all possible data.

The designer of the layout style should consider such aspects as font style, color schemes, highlighting, tables, layers, and so on. When gen-

erating HTML, one can apply CSS in addition to the XSL. Many XML practitioners will leave most of the styling to CSS and use XSL only for its unique capabilities of specifying and reordering data.
Look at an abbreviated version of the style sheet used earlier:

```
<?xml version="1.0"?>
  <xsl:stylesheet
   xmlns:xsl="http://www.w3.org/TR/WD-xsl">
  <xsl:template match="/">
   <xsl:for-each
  select="filmlibrary/motionpicture">
   <xsl:value-of select="title"/>
   <xsl:value-of select="genre"/>
   <xsl:value-of select="year"/>
   </xsl:for-each>
  </xsl:template>
</xsl:stylesheet>
```

The style sheet may include other style sheet modules by one of the statements `xsl:include` or `xsl:import`. These may, in turn, include (or import) other modules, and on down the line it goes. Both of these extend the style sheet tree of the document.

The `xsl:include` element is essential to locating the XSLT document so that the appropriate transformations may be applied. Generally, the `xsl:include` element has syntax similar to the following, which adheres to established practice for URIs:

```
<xsl:include href="http://www.document.org">
```

This directive acts very much like an include file in a language such as C, C++, or Java.

The `xsl:import` element provides the means to import one style sheet module into another and allows style sheets to override each other. Its major difference from `xsl:include` is that the `xsl:import` element is only acceptable as a top-level element. In XSLT version 1.0 (www.w3. org/TR/xslt#import), the W3C states:

... the `xsl: import` element children must precede all other element children of an `xsl:stylesheet` element, including any xsl:include element children. When xsl:include is used to include a style sheet, any xsl:import elements in the included document are moved up in the including document to after any existing xsl:import elements in the including document. .

This simply means that xsl:import is declared before any other child elements (such as xsl:include) and that when xsl:include is used, any xsl:import elements of the included document move up to a position following the xsl:import of the including (original) document. When using include and import, the overall structure of the XSL/XML document will become more sensitive to element ordering, and it is important to pay special attention to the hierarchy of the elements in the document. One cannot overlook errors because they can severely harm the quality of the presentation, and they do so in different ways for different user applications.

Comparison of XSL and CSS

Although the goals of both XSL and CSS have common roots, and on the surface, they appear to accomplish the same result, the power of XSL becomes evident as search patterns become more complex. Although CSS provides some pattern searching, it primarily applies styles to elements and defines rules for the desired rendering of the XML document. CSS is generally applicable mainly to HTML (or XHTML), whereas XSL focuses on XML.

CSS and XSLT are very complementary technologies as opposed to competing ones. Each still has a very prominent place in the XML world. Remember that CSS is a rules-based tool, whereas XSLT is template-based and, as such, can go well beyond simple styling to offer transformations, manipulations, and organization. However, bear in mind that frequently CSS will fit the bill quite nicely when XSLT would be considered overkill. Often HTML authors are more comfortable with CSS, whereas server-side folks (Structured Query Language, or SQL, and scripting types) may prefer XSLT. The choice depends on the circumstances and your preferences.

XSL is the more manipulative and dynamic of the two techniques and performs three primary tasks:

- It transforms an XML document.
- It defines the parts and patterns of an XML document.
- It formats an XML document.

Comparatively, CSS2 does the following:

- It provides selectors for pattern matching.
- It generates a formatting structure based on media type.
- It presents the document based on the UA.
- It transfers the formatting structure to the document tree.

At their most basic common denominators, both XSL and CSS can apply the presentation markup required by a UA to the document source file-whether it is XML or HTML. CSS provides some tools for pattern matching, such as element selection, but XSL surpasses CSS by providing much more complex possibilities. For example, an XSL pattern can select a fragment of a structure, such as the second item of a bulleted list or the sibling of a node for specific style application. CSS would have to accept the entire bulleted list as a selector for the style. Additionally, XSL has comparative operators and the like that can test an element and its contents to determine the validity of the selector.

 **Note!**

CSS is an attractive and simple alternative to XSL unless it is necessary to reorder information or identify information using sophisticated matching.

Whereas CSS properties support specification of a wide range of characteristics for display and rendering of an element, XSL goes beyond decoration to actually interacting with the document structure and provides the necessary formatting and style that the document requires.

XSL accomplishes transformation by joining an XML source document (XML) with an XSL document. It combines the source tree of the XML document with the style tree of the XSL file and produces a result tree.

XSL and CSS share a common goal: the application of styling information that is necessary for document rendering. The two languages accomplish this goal in different ways. CSS uses selectors to indicate the styled element, and each selector provides properties of the style. The syntax for the CSS selector is as follows:

```
selector(property_1; property_2; . . .
;property_n)
```

The CSS selector is usually a standard HTML element such as p or table. In the case of XML, the user-defined (rather than DTD- or schema-defined) elements constitute the selector. Either way works just fine. The properties listed in the selector must be values that the UA can interpret and apply. In the case of a heading color style, it makes the most sense to use either a numeric red-green-blue (RGB) color value or to choose from a standardized color list. (See www.w3. org/TR/html4 / types.html#h-6.5 for the 16 main color names and their corresponding RGB values.) Here is an example of a heading color style:

```
h1 {color: red}
```

Sizes and weights are number-based (and there are many units from which to choose), so there is a smaller margin for misinterpretation than there is with colors. Refer to Chapter 4 for more detail.

XSL uses a different selection system, which is made up of pattern matching and formatting objects that look like the following (notice that all rules for XML well-formed markup apply to XSL just as with any other XML element):

```
<xsl:template match="pattern goes here">
  <formatting object(s) go here/>
</xsl:template>
```

XSL and XSLT

XSL applies styles by incorporating XPath into the pattern statement to specify the element or elements to which the formatting object should apply.

The CSS style element h1 {color: red} would look like this in XSL:

```
<xsl:template match="h1">
 <fo:block color="red">
  <xsl:apply-templates/>
 </fo:block>
</xsl:template>
```

Although this particular example is somewhat complicated for the simple task that it accomplishes, the sophisticated format is necessary to support the complete richness of the general `xsl:template`. For example, the template can replace elements via regular expressions, count them, or reorder them differently, based on their positioning.

XSLT Top-Level Elements

A top-level element in XSLT is any element that can occur as a child to the `xsl:stylesheet` (or its synonym `xsl:transform`) element. The following 12 elements in XSLT are top-level elements:

- `xsl:attribute-set`
- `xsl:decimal-format`
- `xsl:import`
- `xsl:include`
- `xsl:key`
- `xsl:namespace-alias`
- `xsl:output`
- `xsl:param`
- `xsl:preserve-space`
- `xsl:template`
- `xsl:strip-space`
- `xsl:variable`

These are the only elements that an `xsl:stylesheet` (`xsl:transform`) can contain. A style sheet takes the form of the `xsl:stylesheet` element and must contain the version attribute. All other elements are optional.

The bare-bones style sheet declaration is:

```
<xsl:stylesheet: version="number">
.
.
.
</xsl:stylesheet>
```

Typically, more detailed information is present, such as in this example from XSL Transformations (XSLT) version 1. 0, published by the W3C (WWW. w3. org/TR/xstt#stylesheet-element):

```
<xsl:stylesheet version="1.0"
  xmlns:xsl=
  "http://www.w3.org/1999/XSL/Transform">
    <xsl :import href=" . . . " />
    <xsl:include href=" . . . "/>
    <xsl:strip-space elements=" . . . "/>
    <xsl:preserve-space elements=" . . . "/>
    <xsl:output:method=" . . . "/>
    <xsl:key name=" . . . " match=" . . . "
  use=" . . . "/>
    <xsl:decimal-format name=" . . . "/>
    <xsl:namespace-alias
    stylesheet-prefix=" . . . "
    result-prefix=" . . . "/>
    <xsl:attribute-set name=" . . . ">
    .
    .
    .
    </xsl:attribute-set>
    <xsl:variable name=" . . . "> . . . </
    xsl:variable>
    <xsl:param name=" . . . "> . . . </
      xsl:param>
    <xsl:template match=" . . . ">
    .
    .
    .
    </xsl:template>
    <xsl:template name=" . . . ">
    .
    .
    .
```

```
    </xsl:template>
</xsl:stylesheet>
```

The ellipses indicate where the content would go, and again, these are all optional elements, but remember that the `xsl:stylesheet` element must have the version attribute.

Furthermore, the order in which these elements appear in the document is not critical, with the exception of an `import` or `include` statement, which must reside before any references to elements it contains.

Simplified XSLT

Remember that XSL provides formatting objects (that is, instructions) to an XSLT processor (such as Xalan from the Apache group at http://xml.apache.org/), which applies them to the XML source tree, creating a document that the client UA can process as (X)HTML. As far as the UA is concerned (Web browser or PDA), HTML is HTML (or XHTML) whether produced at run time by an XSLT processor or by a static HTTP server. The XSLT process is transparent to the end user, and because a server usually interprets it on the fly, the dynamic document-generation possibilities are tremendous. Specifying the style required via the XSL file allows one to provide the optimal document for a given situation.

The simplified process looks something like that shown in Figure 7-3.

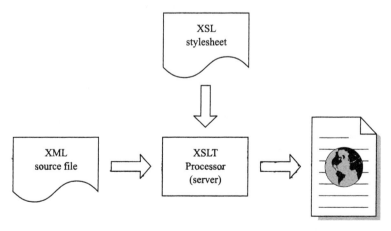

Figure 7-3 The process of applying an XSL style sheet.

The steps involved in this simplified process are

1. Accepting an XML document
2. Accepting an XSL style sheet
3. Creating a result tree from the XML source tree
4. Interpreting the result tree
5. Formatting the output to the UA

The first four steps of the process are collectively called *tree transformation* and the last is called *formatting*. The tree-transformation steps might modify the structure of the result tree from the initial source tree to produce an output that is very different from the original. For example, the result tree might present the material very differently by either reordering, changing, or eliminating information. The formatting applies to the result tree, not the source tree, so one can work within the legal range of modification and then apply the formatting. This process enables highly versatile rendering and conveniently supports the creation of radically diverse variations of the same document.

Consider the example of a quiz whose information sits in an XML document. It might contain 300 questions with answers. If each student group requires 50 questions (and no answers), it is easy to create a result tree of six complete sets of 50 questions each leaving out the answers on the student version and including the answers on the instructor's version. After the tree-transformation process produces the appropriate set of questions and version, the different styles apply their formatting.

If this quiz serves the purpose of classroom testing, the instructor can apply formatting that is appropriate for paper output. If it is a course delivered over the Web, the instructor applies proper formatting for (X)HTML. Another possibility is that the quiz tests students who may suffer a visual impairment or some other special need, so the instructor applies formatting for voice output. All these possibilities use a single XML document, and all the output versions result from simple XSL transformations.

Another alternative is to send both the XML document and the XSLT document to the browser and let the browser do the formatting work. This technique is more along the lines of the CSS method of presentation and depends on the capabilities of the XML rendering engine of the browser. Until recently, XML support in browsers has been limited and rather sparse, so for most documents, server-side formatting has been the best option. This is changing as browsers continue to add features. However, there are bandwidth and security tradeoff between providing all the files to the client versus only what is required to present the document. Most likely, a middle-ground approach is advisable, sharing load and bandwidth. If multiple XML source documents can share a single XSLT file, it might be most efficient to perform the formatting on the browser (client) side. In the case of PDAs and other small devices, it is more efficient to do the formatting on the server. Ideally, either method should yield the same results, with the XSLT file being central to the success of the document presentation.

> # Remember!
>
> At the simplest level, the XSLT process does nothing more than convert XML to HTML (or XHTML).

XSLT Template Bodies

XSL and XSLT use templates to describe how to transform an XML document for presentation. Whereas CSS uses selectors to apply style, XSL uses a match or pattern attribute to designate a style association with a particular document or portion of a document.

Taking a truncated version of the style sheet markup used earlier in this chapter, the template portion is as follows:

```
<xsl:template match="/">
  <xsl:for-each
  select="filmlibrary/motionpicture">
    <xsl:value-of select="title"/>
    <xsl:value-of select="genre"/>
    <xsl:value-of select="year"/>
  </xsl:for-each>
</xsl:template>
```

The match attribute for the template attempts to match the / (root) character (in other words, the whole document), selecting (for-each

as a loop) the nodes filmlibrary/motionpicture and then selecting from those the nodes title, genre, and year and applying
the style to those nodes until the loop ends. The table elements are missing in order to make the example clearer, but if they are returned, the
styling becomes more apparent. The code loops through as instructed and
uses the value found in the node as a dynamic value to be embedded into
or styled by (X)HTML.

Here (as previously presented in the XSLT Transformation Process
section near the beginning of this chapter) is the entire style sheet, templates and all:

```xml
<?xml version="1.0"?>
 <xsl:stylesheet
  xmlns:xsl="http://www.w3.org/TR/WD-xsl">
 <xsl:template match="/">
  <html>
  <head>
   <title>Film Library</title>
  </head>
    <body>
     <table border="2" bgcolor="white">
      <tr>
       <th>Title</th>
       <th>Genre</th>
       <th>Year</th>
      <tr>
      <xsl:for-each
       select="filmlibrary/motionpicture">
      <tr>
       <td><xsl:value-of select=
       "title"/></td>
       <td><xsl:value-of select=
       "genre"/></td>
       <td><xsl:value-of select="year"/></td>
      </tr>
      </xsl:for-each>
     </table>
    </body>
   </html>
```

```
    </xsl:template>
  </xsl:stylesheet>
```

 **Note!**

The fundamental action of an XSLT transform is to transform the matched quantity by sometimes adding text, sometimes deleting text, sometimes simply copying existing text, and sometimes re-ordering text.

XSL Sorting

XSL sorting makes use of the sort element as defined by W3C at http://www.w3.org/TR/xslt#sorting by the syntax:

```
<xsl:sort
  select=string-expression
  lang={ nmtoken }
  data-type={ "text" | "number" |
    qname-but-not-ncname }
  order={ "ascending" | "descending" }
  case-order=
    { "upper-first" | "lower-first" } />
```

Multiple sort elements are acceptable with the first designating the primary sort key, the second the secondary key, and so forth. All xls:sort elements should appear as the first children of an xls:for-each element. The following for-each code generates the same table as the example from the preceding section except that it arranges the rows in ascending order by title.

```
<xsl:for-each
  select="filmlibrary/motionpicture">
<xsl:sort select="title"/>
```

```
<tr>
 <td><xsl:value-of select="title"/></td>
 <td><xsl:value-of select="genre"/></td>
 <td><xsl:value-of select="year"/></td>
</tr>
</xsl:for-each>
```

Attribute Value Templates

One method for adding new elements and attributes at the XSL stage (for output) is through attribute value templates. These templates allow one to convert between attribute and element (and vice versa) or supply either of these with a value derived from a function call or hard-coded statement (such as an SQL statement).

Because the main job of an XSLT processor is to follow the instructions found in the XSLT file, it has convenient access to the result tree as it is being created from the source tree of the XML file and the XSLT style sheet. Templates provide a means to dynamically insert values into the result tree, based on the document flow.

The following example illustrates a common syntax for attribute value templates that create new elements:

```
<xsl:stylesheet
 xmlns:xsl=
  "http://www.w3.org/1999/XSL/Transform"
  version="1.0">
 <xsl:template match="filmlibrary">
  <motionpicture>
   <title>The Wizard of Oz</title>
   <year><xsl-value-of select="/year"/></year>
   <xsl:apply-templates/>
  </motionpicture>
 </xsl:template>
</xsl:stylesheet>
```

When the processor sees a filmlibrary element, it applies this template to create a new motionpicture element using the hard-coded title, *The Wizard of Oz*, and selecting the year element from the filmlibrary to act as the motionpicture element's year. It then copies all markup from the original filmlibrary element to the new motionpicture element.

The role of the xsl:applytemplates element is to assure that the processor applies all appropriate templates to the children of the new motionpicture element after it creates it. The default template for all elements always includes xsl:applytemplates, but there will be no default template applied to the new motionpicture element since another template has created it dynamically.

The following style sheet illustrates how to add attributes to an existing XML element through XSLT:

```
<xsl:stylesheet
 xmlns:xsl=
  "http://www.w3.org/1999/XSL/Transform"
 version="1.0">
 .
 .
 .
 <xsl:template match="title">
  <title
   lead-actor="Frank Morgan"
   lead-actress="Judy Garland"
   director="Victor Fleming">
  </xsl:template>
 .
 .
 .
</xsl:stylesheet>
```

When applied to the data:

```
<motionpicture>
 <title>
  The Wizard of Oz
 </title>
 <year>1939</year>
 <genre category="musical"></genre>
</motionpicture>
```

the above template produces:

```
<motionpicture>
 <title>
  lead-actor="Frank Morgan"
  lead-actress="Judy Garland"
  director="Victor Fleming">
  "The Wizard of Oz"
 </title>
 <year>1939</year>
 <genre category="musical"></genre>
</motionpicture>
```

Notice that the attributes used above are hard-coded. One could use the value returned by a function or a variable value as the attribute value. For example, the following adds the value of variable runtime as an attribute:

```
<xsl:stylesheet
 xmlns:xsl=
  "http://www.w3.org/1999/XSL/Transform"
  version="1.0">
 <xsl:template match="title">
  <title
   lead-actor="Frank Morgan"
   lead-actress="Judy Garland"
   director="Victor Fleming"
   runtime="{@Runtime}">
 </xsl:template>
</xsl:stylesheet>
```

The @Runtime variable is the value of the runtime attribute found in the title element. In the earlier example, the statement

```
<xsl:value-of select="/year"/>
```

indicates that the element year is to be selected, based on the / character. The @ indicates an attribute, and / indicates an element.

About XSL Formatting Objects

XSL formatting objects (sometimes abbreviated as XSL-FOs) are key components of XSL and XSLT, much like selectors are in CSS. Formatting objects are the second main portion of the XSL specification, intended to provide formatting semantics to XML objects during style transformations.

The syntax for XSL-FOs is fairly straightforward, reminiscent of the other XML languages and defined, as usual, at the W3C Web site (www.w3.org/TR/xsl/slice6.html#fo-section). XSL-FOs provide the vocabulary needed to describe layout, styling, and other presentation markup in great detail while maintaining separation from the XML source. Formatting objects are applied during XSLT processing, and even though they can be very complex and verbose at times, the syntactical rules are similar to those presented previously.

In addition to (simple) formatting objects, FOP is available from *Apache*. FOP is intended primarily for the printing output of documents-hence the P at the end of the acronym. Frequently, the output is a PDF document, but most of the concepts between FO and FOP are similar.

Like all XML documents, the XSL-FO file begins with an XML declaration and root element:

```
<?xml version="1.0" encoding="utf-8"?>
<fo:root>
.
.
.
</fo:root>
```

Following this initial declaration is the remainder of the XSL-FO file, which consists of:

- A master set for the layout, made up of: descriptions of the kind of pages to be found in the document and the sequencing of the formats used in those pages
- The pages themselves.

The master set for the document layout is a series of XSL-FO elements starting with the fo:layout-master-set element immediately after the `fo:root` element. The model for XSL-FO uses the concept of *areas*, which are collections of rectangular regions that contain the text, images, white space, and other layout components. There are more than 50 elements associated with formatting objects, and each of them uses the areas model.

The formatting objects differ primarily in the type of content they represent, whether it is a block of text, a list, or a table. The XSL-FO areas are composed of these main groups (see www.w3.org/TR/xsl / slice6.html#fo-section):

- Declaration, pagination, and layout formatting objects
- Block formatting objects
- In-line formatting objects
- Table formatting objects
- List formatting objects
- Link and multi-formatting objects
- Out-of-line formatting objects
- Other formatting objects

A document (or the master set) consists of collections of these areas and objects that ultimately describe the page. The full list of XSL-FO elements is available at the W3C Web site but some of the common ones are

- `fo:block` defines a `block` region, similar to XHTML's `blockquote`.
- `fo:flow` contains the flowing text object that becomes pages.
- `fo:initial-property-set` specifies formatting properties for the first line of an `fo:block`.
- `fo:inline` formats a portion of text with a background or encloses it within a border.
- `fo:layout-master-set` is the main wrapper for all master elements.
- `fo:page-sequence-master` specifies sequences of page masters that help to generate pages.
- `fo:region-body` specifies the area located in the center of the `fo:simple-page-master` region.
- `fo:root` is the top node of an XSL result tree of formatting objects.

- `fo:simple-page-master` specifies the geometry of the page.

Of course, there are many tags, each of which provides specific formatting and style. An example of the use and syntax of the FO, modified from the W3C XSL Recommendation (at www.w3.org/TR/xsl/slice6.html#section-N13277-Inline-level-Formatting-Objects) should help:

```
<text>
<p>This is the text of a paragraph that is going
to be presented with the first line in
small-caps.</p>
</text>
```

The XSL style sheet, keying on the p element, is

```
<?xml version="1.0"?>
<xsl:styesheet
 xmlns:xsl=
  "http://www.w3.org/1999/XSL/Transform"
 xmlns:fo="http://www.w3.org/1999/XSL/Format"
version="1.0">
<xsl:template match="p">
 <fo:block>
  <fo-initial-property-set
   font-variant="small-caps"/>
  <xsl:apply-templates/>
< /fo:block>
</xsl:template>
</xsl:stylesheet>
```

When applied to the xml markup that precedes it, this derives the result tree instance:

```
<fo:block>
 <fo-initial-property-set
  font-variant="small-caps">
 </fo-initial-property-set>
 This is the text of a paragraph that is going
```

```
to be presented with the first line in
small-caps.
</fo:block>
```

Remember

Formatting objects provide a means of specifying detailed formatting information within XSL transforms.

Review Questions

Review Question 7.1 What are the three trees used in XSL Transformations?

   a. Source tree
   b. Result tree
   c. Instruction tree
   d. Information tree

Answer: a, b, and c

Review Question 7.2 Put these steps in the correct order.

   a. A tree is handed off to an XSLT processor.
   b. The tree is output to a UA in a format such as HTML, speech, or text.
   c. An XML parser interprets the provided XML document and forms a tree.
   d. When the XSLT processor finds a match, it outputs a tree fragment (result tree)
   e. The XSLT processor compares the nodes in the tree with the instructions contained in the referenced style sheet (XSL).

Answer: The correct order is c, a, e, d, and b.

Review Question 7.3 Which of the following docs CSS use to establish what receives styling?

   a. Rules
   b. XPath

    c. Templates
    d. Tags
Answer: a. CSS uses rules to define styling.

Review Question 7.4 Which of the following does XSL use to establish what receives styling?
    a. Rules
    b. XPath
    c. Templates
    d. Tags
Answer: c. XSL uses templates to define styling.

Review Question 7.5 In what must the style sheet declaration be included?
    a. The XML source document
    b. The directory tree
    c. The CSS file
    d. The output file
Answer: a

Review Question 7.6 Which of the following are advantages that XSL offers over CSS?
    a. Document manipulation
    b. Convenience
    c. Defines parts of a document
    d. Formats a document
Answer: a, c, and d

Review Question 7.7 Name four datatypes used in XSL and XSLT.
Answer: The most common datatypes used in XSL and XSLT are:
    String
    Number
    Boolean
    Node set
    Tree

Review Question 7.8 XSL and XSLT datatypes are strongly-cast. True or false?
Answer: False

Review Question 7.9 Which of the following are expressions in XSL?
    a. Pattern
    b. Function call
    c. Match
    d. Select
    e. All of the above
Answer: e

Review Question 7.10 These are all FOs. True or false?
   • Declaration, pagination, and layout formatting objects
   • Block formatting objects
   • In-line formatting objects
   • Table formatting objects
   • List formatting objects
   • Link and multi=formatting objects
   • Out-of-line formatting objects
   • Other formatting objects
Answer: True

Solved Problem

Solved Problem 7.1 Using the example in the "XSL Sorting" section, create the changes needed to sort the fields:
    a. Left to right as year, genre, and title
    b. In order by year (descending) and title (alphabetical).
Here is the loop used before:
```
<xsl:for-each
 select="filmlibrary/motionpicture">
<xsl:sort select="title"/>
<tr>
 <td><xsl:value-of select="title"/></td>
 <td><xsl:value-of select="genre"/></td>
 <td><xsl:value-of select="year"/></td>
</tr>
</xsl:for-each>
```
Answer:
    a. ```
       <xsl:for-each
          select="filmlibrary/motionpicture">
          <xsl:sort select="title"/>
       ```
       ```

```
<tr>
 <td><xsl:value-of select="year"/></td>
 <td><xsl:value-of select="genre"/></td>
 <td><xsl:value-of select="title"/></td>
</tr>
</xsl:for-each>
```

b.
```
<xsl:for-each
  select="filmlibrary/motionpicture">
<xsl:sort select="year" order="descending"/>
<xsl:sort select="title"/>
<tr>
 <td><xsl:value-of select="title"/></td>
 <td><xsl:value-of select="genre"/></td>
 <td><xsl:value-of select="year"/></td>
</tr>
</xsl:for-each>
```

Chapter 8
XPOINTER
AND XLINK

Extending Xpath

The XPath technology, as discussed in Chapters 6 and 7, does not locate information through *string matching*, define address *points* and *ranges*, define address *nodes*, or use XPath in URI references to locate *addresses*.

XPointer is an extension to Xpath that addresses these shortcomings. XPointer extends XPath in a number of ways without negating any of the XPath functionality and syntax. Extensions in XPointer add the following to XPath (derived from a list at www.w3.org/TR/WD-xptr#b2d 250b5b9):

- Two new location types, namely, point and range. These correspond to Document Object Model (DOM) positions and ranges (see Chapter 5).
- A generalization of the in-place XPath concepts of nodes, node types, and node sets. These are added to the locations concept of XPointer.
- Rules for an XPath evaluation context.
- The functions `string-range()`, `range()`, and `range-`

148

`to();` `here()` and `origin();` and `start-point()`and
`end point()`.

These extensions add the extra dimensions needed to create a framework for tools and methods to XML (and ultimately) the Web.

Using XPointers

Because XPointer extends XPath, most of the XPath concepts and methods carry over into XPointer. There are, of course, small and subtle differences, as one would expect, but for the most part, XPointer will be familiar in scope and syntax. The conditions in which XPointer should be applied are in cases such as the following:

- Using string matching to locate information
- Appending URIs for added flexibility and versatility to links
- Addressing a portion of a document node instead of the entire node.

XPointer string matching can apply to the motion picture example XML from previous chapters. For this example, however, let's change the `category` attribute to an element to make the search a little easier:

```
<?xml version=1.0?>
<?xml-stylesheet type="text:xsl"
 href="filmlibrary.xsl"?>
<filmlibrary>
 <motionpicture>
  <title>"The Wizard of Oz"</title>
  <year>1939</year>
  <genre
   <category>
    musical
   </category>
  </genre>
 </motionpicture>
 <motionpicture>
  <title>"Duck Soup"</title>
  <year>1933</year>
```

```
<genre
 <category>
  comedy
 </category>
 </genre>
</motionpicture>
<motionpicture>
 <title>"Gone With the Wind"</title>
 <year>1939</year>
 <genre
  <category>
   drama
  </category>
 </genre>
</motionpicture>
</filmlibrary>
```

This example searches for the substring drama, which resides in the genre and category elements. This allows one to identify any films that are dramas and ignore the others. The example uses function string-range(), a basic function that allows simple string matching using a syntax reminiscent of most XML functions. The string-range() function takes two arguments, a node set to search and the desired substring, and returns a range of node sets that contain the substring; therefore, the following says to start at the document root (/) and return node sets containing the substring drama:

```
xpointer(string-range(/,"drama"))
```

Recall the characters (axes) used in expressions to define node context (and node sets): / is root node, // is descendant (or self) node, comma (,) is the self-node, and period (.) is the parent node.

If one were interested in the substring only when it resided directly in, or as a descendent of, a genre node, the syntax would be as follows:

```
xpointer(string-range(//genre, "drama"))
```

This also would return node sets in the children of genre (in this case, category). To limit the search to the node sets in just genre, the statement would change to the following:

```
xpointer(string-range(.genre, "drama"))
```

Applying this function to the search for a particular year would start at root to return `title`, `genre`, and so on, as well as the year. Therefore, the following returns two node sets as a result: the set containing `"The Wizard of Oz"` and the set containing `"Gone With the Wind"` because both of them have 1939 in the year element:

```
xpointer(string-range (/,"1939"))
```

The `string-range()` function also can return subsets of the result set. The position of the node in the result set can be specified by `position()`=n. To return the first occurrence of the year "1939" in the document (starting at /), the function(s) would be expressed as follows:

```
xpointer(string-range(/,"1939") [position()=1])
```

Basic XLinks

XLink expands on the familiar practice of hyperlinks found in (X)HTML and XML. Recall that (X)HTML hyperlinks have the following characteristics:

- They are one-directional; a document can link only one way from reference to referenced.
- Links are embedded into the (X)HTML; they are part of the document.
- Links may target a portion of the (X)HTML document, but they still access the entire document, not just the requested fragment.
- (X)HTML links can refer only to two resources. The first one is the calling document (the one that contains the hyperlink), and the other is the target document,

With the expanded possibilities of XLink, each of the limitations just noted can be resolved as follows:

- One can specify multiple traversal directions between resources, avoiding the one-way constraint.
- A hyperlink can specify part of an external document, in the same fashion as XSL.

- Using XPointer along with XLink allows linking of a fragment of the document as a subset of the entire document.
- Links can include multiple resources, not just the two that (X)HTML can reference.

XLink contains several attributes that supplement the traditional (X)HTML hyperlink:

- The attribute href is (still) used in XLink.
- One can provide a type attribute, specifying the type of XLink being created.
- The role attribute specifies the resource (in an extended link) in a machine-readable format.
- The title attribute specifies the resource (in an extended link) in a human-readable format.
- The show attribute specifies the fashion in which the resource shall be displayed.

The Web page at http://www.w3.org/TR/xlink/ holds numerous examples of Xlink usage.

Review Questions

Review Question 8.1 Why does XPointer offer extensions to XPath?
   a. To locate information via string matching
   b. To define points and ranges
   c. To define nodes
   d. To define locations
   e. All of the above
Answer: e.

Review Question 8.2 List two parameters of the `string-range()` function.
Answer: The search node and the search string.

Review Question 8.3 What conditions are ideal for XPointer?
   a. The need to use string-matching to locate information.
   b. The need to append URIs
   c. The need to address a portion of the document
   d. All of the above
Answer: d.

Review Question 8.4 With what media types will XPointer work?
   a. text/xml
   b. text/html
   c. application/xml
   d. text/xml-external-parsed-entity
Answer: a, c and d.

Review Question 8.5 Which two of these are functions of XPointer?
   a. `string-range()`
   b. `here()`
   c. `now()`
   d. `parent()`
Answer: a, b.

Review Question 8.6 Is a point more than one location?
Answer: No, a point is a place in the document consisting of a single character or a single node.

Review Question 8.7 What is a range?
   a. An area between two points
   b. An area specified by nodes
   c. An area at the beginning of the document
   d. An area between elements
Answer: a.

Review Question 8.8 What is a location?
   a. A node in the document
   b. A node that includes points and ranges
   c. An element made up of points
   d. Part of an axis
Answer: b.

Review Question 8.9 What is a location set?
   a. A collection of points,
   b. Points and nodes
   c. A collection of locations
   d. Pairs of points
Answer: c.

Review Question 8.10 Name two axis nodes.

Answer: Any two of these: child, parent, self, ancestor, ancestor-or-self, attribute, descendant, descendant-or-self, following, following-sibling, namespace, preceding, preceding-sibling

Review Question 8.11 What conditions are ideal for XPointer?
   a. The need to use string-matching to locate information
   b. The need to append URIs
   c. The need to address a portion of the document
   d. All of the above
Answer: d. All of the above.

Review Question 8.12 XPointer uses the system of axes, predicates and functions? True or false?
Answer: True.

Review Question 8.13 Does XPointer use the same location path characters as XPath?
Answer: Yes.

Appendix A
GLOSSARY

absolute location path In XPath, the path for the location that starts at the document root.

action The portion of a construction rule that describes how a document element (pattern) should be formatted.

API (application programming interface) A specific collection of programming instructions that allows one program to invoke the functions of a second program (generally an application requesting services from the operating system).

ASCII (American Standard Code for Information Interchange) A method of coding characters for translation. Characters can include numbers, text, and symbols, which are rendered into digital form. ASCII includes only 127 characters and is only really useful for Latin-based languages.

attribute A named characteristic associated with an XML element that supplies additional data about an element.

attribute-list declaration A DTD listing of which attributes can be combined with a given element. A listing declaration includes the names of the attributes, their values and defaults (if applicable), and whether the attribute is required or optional.

attribute type The value that specifies whether an attribute is a string, tokenized, or enumerated attribute.

attribute value A list of all the possible values available for an attribute.

axis The first section of each location path step in XPath, which specifies the correlation between a context node and the nodes chosen by the step.

bidirectional link An XLink convention that allows a hyperlink to be navigated in more than one direction.

box properties A group of CSS properties and values for an element that governs the element's margins, padding, height, width, and border aspects.

character entity A series of characters used to correspond to other characters; for example, < and " show a string of characters (lt and Egrave) that stand for other characters (> and Ú).

character reference Text used in a document to create declarations, markup, and text inside XML elements.

character set A collection of values that map to a specific symbol set or alphabet.

child element An element that is nested within another element; such an element also can be a parent of other, lower-level elements.

classification properties A CSS property and value grouping that controls how white space and lists are presorted.

comments Notations in an XML document that are ignored by the XML processor.

content-based markup Markup that describes information so that it can be processed by one or more applications or delivered aurally or in Braille.

content identifier A token that uniquely distinguishes any piece of data or content.

CSS (Cascading Style Sheets) A method of coding for defining how certain Hypertext Markup Language (HTML), dynamic HTML (DHTML), or XML elements, such as paragraphs and headings, should be displayed.

declaration Specific markup that provides special instructions to the XML processor for how to process a document.

document element The most important component of an XML document, the document element contains all the text and markup in the document. (Also called the *root element.*)

document type declaration A piece of data that informs the processor of the DTD's location and contains declarations for a document. Also called the DOCTYPE declaration.

DOM (Document Object Model) A programming interface that is platform-and-language-neutral and that provides programs and scripts with access to the content, structure, and style of documents via a standard method.

DTD (Document Type Definition) A specification for a document used to arrange structural elements and mark-up definitions so that they can be used to create documents.

EDI (Electronic Data Interchange) An official standard used for the electronic exchange of basic business information.

element A document component that consists of markup and the text contained within the markup.

element content model A method for including a specification regarding child elements in element declarations.

element type A named element, such as <Book> or <Title>.

element type declaration A description of an element type and its content within the DTD.

extended link A link stored in an external file that can have relationships with more than two resources.

font properties CSS properties and values that specify font information for document elements.

HTML (Hypertext Markup Language) A markup language used to create Web pages for display on the Internet or an intranet.

HTTP (Hypertext Transfer Protocol) The Web protocol that provides communication between a Web server and a Web browser (uses HTML).

hypertext A method for linking document locations. By clicking on a hypertext element, a user is sent to another location that can be within the same document or another Web document.

inheritance The process of a child or sibling element being assigned (inheriting) the characteristics assigned to the parent element.

in-line styles Styles that are applicable to an XML document element.

internal DTD subset The piece of a document's DTD included within a document.

intranet An private, internal network that uses Internet protocols and standards.

ISO-Latin-I The default character set used by XML and HTML. (Also known as ISO 8859-1.)

Java Sun Microsystems' object-oriented programming language used for Web application development.

Java class files The file or set of files containing instructions for a Java applet or application.

JavaScript A scripting language used on Web pages.

metadata Literally, data about data. Specifically, metadata contain defined elements for describing a document's structure, content, or rendering.

metalanguage A language, such as XML and SGML, that communicates information about the language itself. Metalanguages are used to create other languages.

MIME (Multipurpose Internet Mail Extensions) An e-mail standard that allows messages to include multiple types of data (such as binary, audio, video, and graphics) as attachments. MIME types also identify document types during transfers over the Web.

MSXML (Microsoft XML) Microsoft's XML parser for Internet Explorer.

multidirectional link A link that can be traversed in more than one direction.

namespace A set of element types and attribute names.

nesting The process of elements containing other elements in a hierarchical form.

node A portion of an XML tree structure.

node-set function An XPath function used in location paths to define the members of a node set.

notation An XML declaration that connects a type of unparsed entity, such as a JPEG image, with a processing application, such as a graphics program.

notation declaration Information that associates a notation name with data to identify an information interpreter described by the notation.

numeric entity A set of numbers used to represent a character. Numeric entities are identified by an ampersand followed by a pound sign (#). (Also called *character references.*)

parameter entity A DTD entity used to create an alias for a group of elements in the DTD.

parent element An element that contains child elements,

parsed entity Character data assigned as content for an entity name.

parser An application that breaks an XML document into an element tree and checks its syntax.

PCDATA (parsed character data) Plain-text element content.

PDF (Portable Document Format) Adobe Systems' graphics file format that requires the Adobe Acrobat Reader, PageMaker, or Photoshop for display.

Perl A common graphic interface programming language.

presentation-based markup Markup, such as HTML, that describes text to be rendered by a browser.

pull technology A method for a browser to retrieve information from a Web server.

push technology A method for initiating content delivery from a server to a client.

RDF (Resource Description Framework) An XML vocabulary for describing Internet resources, which provides a mechanism for organizing, describing, and navigating Web sites.

remote resource A resource, such as a document, image, or sound file, at a location other than the document that contains the link.

result tree The structure of elements and element content in a document.

root element An XML element that is equivalent to the <html> element in HTML. Also called the document element.

schema A pattern for representing the data's model that defines the elements (or objects), their attributes (or properties), and the relationships among the elements.

scripting language A programming language for creating Web page scripts that controls various elements of the page, such as the user interface, styles, and markup.

selector One part of a CSS style rule that defines the markup element to which the style rule is applied.

SGML (Standard Generalized Markup Language) A text-based metalanguage for describing document content and structure,

simple link A link in XML that uses the href attribute to point to a resource.

source tree The structure of elements and element content in an XSLT document.

SQL (Structured Query Language) IBM's language for relational database communications.

style rule An XML document directive that specifies a pattern and an action to take when the specified pattern is found.

style sheet A template-style document that provides information about the organization and content of another document or set of documents,

template The directives in an XSLT style sheet that manage how an element and its content are converted.

text properties CSS properties and values that detail text specifics for document elements.

traversal Using a link in XLink to access a resource.

tree structure A pyramid-shaped organizational scheme that is hierarchical.

Unicode character set The ISOJED 10646 standard 16-bit character encoding scheme. Unicode includes standard Roman and Greek alphabets, as well as mathematical symbols, special punctuation, and non-Roman alphabets, including Hebrew, Chinese, Arabic, Hangul, and other ideographic character sets.

UNIX An interactive time-sharing operating system that is one of the most powerful multi-user operating systems available.

unparsed entity A resource that is not XML-encoded, such as audio and video files (which are binary entities).

URI (Uniform Resource Identifier) A character string that identifies the type and location of an Internet resource.

valid XML document A document that adheres to its DTD and is well formed.

validating parser An application that checks an XML document for validity, it checks the document's DTD or schema and whether the document conforms to it.

VBScript (Visual Basic Scripting Edition) Microsoft's scripting language, similar to Visual Basic. VBScript is used only in Microsoft Web products.

W3C (World Wide Web Consortium) The association that is responsible for developing Web standards.

well-formed document An XML document that goes by the rules established in the XML specification that outline what makes a document well formed.

white space Certain blank areas of a document created by spaces or paragraphs that do not contain text or graphics.

XHTML (Extensible Hypertext Markup Language) The current recommendation from the W3C for merging HTML version 4 (for the vocabulary of elements) and XML (for syntax).

XLink (XML Linking Language) A language in XML documents that established instructions that describe the links among objects.

XML (Extensible Markup Language) A system for defining, validating, and sharing document formats.

XML application An XML implementation that is a DTD or set of DTDs designed to serve a specific purpose. (Also known as an *XML vocabulary.*)

XML declaration Information that informs the processor about which XML version to use for processing an XML document, which details the type of character encoding to be used for the document and whether the XML document is a standalone document.

XML entity Characters that allow a viewer to present a symbol yet not interpret it as markup.

XML namespace A prefix identifier that links an XML markup element to a specific DTD.

XML processor An application for reading and editing XML documents.

XMIL Schema A method of describing XML markup using XML notation.

XML specification A depiction that details how elements are declared and how XML must be constructed for XML processors (which interpret XML code) to process the XML information properly and send it to the Web browser for display.

XPath (XML Path Language) A language used by both XSL and XLInk to address parts of XML documents.

XPointer (XML Pointer Language) A method of designating various resources by using terms that specify locations in documents or resources. XPointer is a companion to Xlink.

XSL (Extensible Stylesheet Language) A style sheet procedure customized for XML.

XSLT (XSL Transformations) An XSL component that provides a language for changing one XML document into another.

Appendix B
ONLINE
RESOURCES

This appendix is a compilation of various online resources for XML.

CSS (Cascading Style Sheets)
Cascading Style Sheets: *http://www.w3.org/Style/CSS/*
Cascading Style Sheets, Level 2:
http://www.w3.org/TR/REC-CSS2/
CSS3 module text:
http://ww.w3.org/TR/2001/WD-css3-text-20010517/

DOM
Document Object Model (DOM):
http://www.oasis-open.org/cover/dom.html
DOM views: *http://www.w3.org/TR/2000/REC-DOM-Level-2-Views-20001113/views.html*
Content models and validation; *http://www.w3.org/TR/2001/WD DOM-Level-3-CMLS-20010209/content-models.html*
DOM core: *http://www.w3.org/TR/2000/REC-DOM-Level-2-Core-20001113/core.html*
DOM activity statement: *http://www.w3.org/DOM/Activity*

General XML
Links to the Recommendations and World Wide Web Consortium
(W3C) documents: *http://www.w3.org/*
XML developer news from XMLhack: *http://www.xmlhack.com*
Café con Leche XML news and resources: *http://www.ibiblio.org/xml/*
A warehouse of XML information:
http://xml.startkabel.nl

Schemas
SCHEMA.NET: *http://www.schema.net*
XML Schema Part 0 primer: *http://www.w3.org/TR/xmlschema-0/*
XML Schema Part I structures: *http: //www.w3. org/TR/xmlschema-1/*
XML Schema Part 2 datatypes: *http: //www.w3. org/TR/xmlschema-2/*
Metadata at W3C http: //www.w3.org/Metadata/

Tools and Tutorials
Free XML tools and software.
http://www.garshol.priv.no/download/xmltools/
W3Schools online web tutorials: *http: / /www. w3schools. com/*
ZVON.org tutorials: *http:/ /www: zvon.org/index*.php

XPath
XQuery 1.0 and XPath 2.0 data model:
http://www.w3.org/TR/2001/WD-query-datamodel-20010607

XSL and XSLT
The Extensible Stylesheet Language (XSL).
http://www.w3.crg/Style/XSL/
XSL Transformations (XSLT) version I.I:
http://www.w3.org/TR/xs1tII/

Appendix C
BIBLIOGRAPHY

GENERAL XML

Beginning XML, by David Hunter. Wrox Press, Birmingham, U.K., 2000, ISBN 1-861-0034-1-2.

Essential XML Beyond Markup, by Don Box, Aaron Skonnard, and John Lam. Addison-Wesley, Upper Saddle River, NJ, 2000, ISBN 0-201-70914-7.

XML A Primer, 2d ed, by Simon St. Laurent. M & T Books, Foster City, CA, 1999, ISBN 0-764-53310-X.

XML Black Book, 2d ed., by Natanya Pitts. Coriolis Group, Scottsdale, AZ, 2001, ISBN1-576-10783-3.

XML By Example, by Benoit Marchal. Que Books, Indianapolis, IN, 2000, ISBN 0-789-72242-9.

The XML Companion, by Neil Bradley. Addison-Wesley, Upper Saddle River, NJ, 2000, ISBN 0-201-67486-6.

XML Elements of Style, by Simon St. Laurent. McGraw-Hill, New York, 2000, ISBN 0-07-212220-X.

XML in a Nutshell, by Elliote Rusty Harold and W. Scott Means. O'Reilly & Associates, Sebastopol, CA, 2001, ISBN 0-596-00058-8.

OTHER XML LANGUAGES

Professional XML Schemas, by Cagle et al. Wrox Press, Birmingham, U.K., 2001, ISBN 1-86100-547-4.

The XSL Companion, by Neil Bradley. Addison-Wesley, Upper Saddle River, NJ, 2000, ISBN 0-201-67487-4.

XSLT Programmer's Reference, by Michael Kay. Wrox Press, Birmingham, U.K., 2000, ISBN 1-86100-312-9.

XSLT Working with XML and HTML, by Khun Yee Fung. Addison-Wesley, Upper Saddle River, NJ, 2000, ISBN 0-201-71103-6.

Index

167